PAT CASH
My Story

Bruce Matthews

Macdonald
Queen Anne Press

A Queen Anne Press BOOK

First published in 1987 in Australia by Penguin Books
Australia

Published in Great Britain in 1988 by
Queen Anne Press, a division of
Macdonald & Co (Publishers) Ltd
3rd Floor
Greater London House
Hampstead Road
London
NW1 7QX

A member of Maxwell Pergamon Publishing
Corporation plc

British Library Cataloguing in Publication Data

Matthews, Bruce
Pat Cash: my story.
1. Lawn tennis. Cash, Pat. Biographies
I. Title II. Cash, Pat
796.342'092'4

ISBN 0-356-15825-X

Printed and bound in Great Britain by Purnell Book
Production Ltd, a member of BPCC plc, Paulton.

Contents

1 Who is Pat Cash?

To attain an accurate measure of Pat Cash's physical condition and specific needs, fitness adviser Ann Quinn drove him mercilessly through a series of tests last summer. One of those torturous trials on a sweltering Melbourne day was a standard start sprint from a laser beam line to another 10 metres away. To Quinn's satisfaction, Cash was timed as the second fastest ever to take the test. At 1.710 seconds he was only one hundredth of a second behind Australia's Olympic hockey goalkeeper Neil Snowden. In stark contrast the sweat-stained tennis star was furious, but he contained the frustration until the exhausting five-hours workout was finished. 'Can I have another go at that sprint test?' Cash enquired. 'I think I can do better this time.' Time didn't permit as technicians at the Phillip Institute in Bundoora had dismantled equipment.

Snowden's record stood – for the time, anyway – and Quinn's helpers had a first-hand knowledge of Cash's iron will to win. It's the stamp of determination bordering on fanaticism that drives sportsmen and women to extraordinary feats of class and endurance and which has earned the stocky Australian deep respect for his craft. Quinn has no doubt Cash will lower the fastest time for that acceleration sprint the next time she allows him near the equipment. He had stepped off a flight from London only the day prior to those workouts last November.

What the tests also revealed was a remarkably well-conditioned young man with the physical capacity to endure the most protracted tennis battle. For instance, his body fat was 4.2 percent compared with 10 percent for a top athlete and 15 to 17 percent for the average male. Really, his outstanding results came as no surprise for Quinn who recalled the physical potential when she had tested him five years earlier. At the age of 16 he was pitted in similar fitness trials against older Australian circuit players, Peter McNamara, Warren Maher, John Trickey and Ernie Ewert. At the time McNamara was Australia's No. 1 player and ranked in the world's top ten. The teenager was faster and stronger than anyone in the group.

Quinn, who has a master's degree in biomechanics and exercise physiology, was there when that super-fitness peaked on the first Sunday in July. She was part of the dedicated team behind Cash's push to become the first Australian to win the Wimbledon men's singles crown since John Newcombe in 1971. While father, Pat senior, supervises the managerial requirements, coach Ian Barclay is in charge of the on-court preparations, sports psychologist Jeff Bond controls the emotions and Quinn tones the body. Daily training to supplement the hours spent on the practice court includes speed, agility and endurance work. The program depends on the tournament court surface and climatic conditions of the particular city on the international tennis circuit. 'All the time you have to hold him back, he wants to go out and do everything better,' Quinn said.

Cash's competitive verve was inherited from his footballer father, Pat and the stubborn independence from Chicago-born mother, Dorothy, who both enjoyed playing social tennis near their North Ringwood home in Melbourne's outer eastern suburbs. Young Patrick was encouraged to have a hit and the Cash family decided to take him to Barclay at nearby Heatherdale Tennis Club to develop the strokes nurtured by previous coaches Bill Mattea and Will Coghlan. At the time, Barclay, a commercial artist turned tennis coach, had a crop of promising juniors. They included Anne and Elizabeth Minter and a talented left-hander named Mark Hartnett, who had already attracted sufficient interest for Newcombe to agree to hit with him on a visit to Melbourne. Understandably, Barclay can still vividly remember the time he first laid a critical tennis gaze on a tiny 11-year-old who one day would realise his Wimbledon dream. 'His father brought him down to seek my appraisal. He had a lot of ability and was virtually a died-in-the-wool baseliner. I don't think he had ventured to the net in his life,' Barclay recalled. Cash's basic tennis education had been on en-tout-cas courts, in those days the most popular surface for tennis clubs in Melbourne's often unpredictable weather. The shifting brick-dust is not dissimilar to the slow clay courts of Europe and requires reliable ground strokes and patience.

Barclay agreed to take on young Cash. Pat immediately fell into friendship with Hartnett who was a year older. 'From that day on he worked his butt off. He was too small to serve and volley but I soon had trouble keeping him away from the net, such was his natural instinct to attack,' Bar-

Pat Cash sr, Pat Cash jr and Dorothy Cash *

clay said. 'Pat and Mark were such little fellows that, to keep them away from the net, I used to jokingly point out that there was enough room to drive a truck down the sidelines past them, let alone a tennis ball.'

Watch Cash's power game based on a solid serve, punishing smash and deep volleys and it's difficult to imagine that such a style was once so totally and frustratingly alien to him. When Barclay first started to develop the strokes, volleying and the smash didn't come naturally and coach and pupil spent many tedious hours trying to get his feet into the correct position.

In particular, Barclay still shudders on recalling the 'horrendous' attempts to learn to hit an overhead merely into court. One day that will live forever with the coach was when Dorothy Cash brought her son to the tennis club during work to install two more courts. 'The graders had levelled the ground exposing the clay and Dorothy had on a pair of old boots. I was feeding balls to Pat and if he top-edged one, he top-edged a dozen over the fence

Ian Barclay, Mark Hartnett and Pat Cash (Photo: *Melbourne Age*)

Mark Hartnett, Ian Barclay and Pat Cash 1981 *

and, plop, into the mud.' As Mrs Cash squelched through the sticky mire to collect the errant balls, her son yelled 'another one, Mum, another one, Mum,' as they flew off the racquet frame. As young Cash gathered the sprayed tennis balls at the end of each lesson, he would breathlessly ask 'is it getting better, Mr B', to which Barclay would reply that they would work, not until they got it right, but until it was perfect.

'I still remember the days when I would see this little face bob up out of the bushes while I was working with a group of mid-week ladies at the club,' Barclay said. Often the youngster would be in uniform from wagging school. "Can we hit, Mr B? I've got to get this smash right," Cash would say as he pestered the club coach until he relented.

Barclay knew he had potential champions in Cash and Hartnett and made financial sacrifices to take them to country tournaments and interstate for the necessary match experience. He would bundle the eager squad of girls and boys into the Ford sedan and roll up the highway to faraway tournaments. With Cash and Hartnett developing into a formidable doubles combination and capturing national age-group singles titles, the coach realised he had exhausted all avenues for advancement in Australia.

To test his youngsters against lads of comparable age in other countries, Barclay sought financial assistance. Arthur Liddle, Dunlop-Slazenger's Victoria manager and Garry Daly, executive director of the Confederation of Australian Sport, were the first approached and the wheels were put into motion. Subsequent meetings eventually formed a group of businessmen into a MATCH syndicate – Make A Tennis Champion Here – in 1978. Cash was then a raw but developing 14-year-old and his dapper coach wanted to gauge his progress against the European claycourters. The first trip the following year was financially underwritten by the syndicate members – Barclay; Pat Cash senior; his brother Leo Cash who was secretary-treasurer; Liddle; Daly; John Bee, CBA bank executive; Peter Thorpe, Simpson's sports clothing managing director; Kevin Turtle, national promotions officer of Australian Airlines (then TAA); and Michael Edgley, entrepreneur and tennis buff. Pat Cash senior, a lawyer, set up a non-profit corporate structure for MATCH syndicate and the junior development squad, though no-one officially called it such, was off to tackle Europe.

The first squad consisted of Hartnett, then the country's top junior; Cash; the Minter sisters and Wally Masur with later teams including players such as John Frawley. Over the next three years the syndicate spent $63,000, modest by modern fiscal standards, flying its squad to junior tournaments in Europe and the US with coach, equipment and a lot of dreams. Its dividend has been substantial: a share in a Wimbledon, a junior Wimbledon, two US junior singles, a French junior singles, a junior US doubles, two Davis Cups, two Avvenire Cups and a Galea Cup (both European junior teams events), 11 grand prix titles and at least 27 Australian titles. Barclay believed the scheme succeeded so gloriously because, unlike other later junior development systems, it did not take the youngsters out of the security of their home environments.

The MATCH syndicate eventually outlived its usefulness and was broken up. The kids grew up, the syndicate members moved on. Daly is now secretary-general of the International Assembly of National Organisations in Sport, Bee is a partner in a Swiss-based firm and Thorpe is the Melbourne distributor for Diadora. Sadly, Liddle, the man who started it all, died of cancer the day after Cash won Wimbledon. Barclay made it back to Melbourne just in time for the funeral two days later.

The Avvenire Cup, Milan 1981 *

The remains of the syndicate had a cheerful reunion at a Chinese restaurant in Melbourne three weeks after the Wimbledon championships to retell the story behind the story. Together they celebrated, marvelled, reminisced and gloated just a little. Daly produced a record of Barclay's expenses on the first trip to Italy, read some of it aloud and everyone laughed. The budget for the first year for fares and expenses was $28,000. Barclay spent a moment mourning the passing of the uncomplicated days of the overworked and often overloaded Ford Fairlane. Everyone said a silent prayer for Liddle who, no doubt, was there in spirit.

Despite the syndicate backing, Italy wasn't exactly all lasagna and frascati for the embattled Barclay who had to pay a coach to fulfil coaching commitments at home and borrow money to take his wife Jackie on the European jaunts. 'There's no price you could put on it. I was earning $400 a week and it was probably costing $1000,' Barclay said.

When young Cash returned from that first overseas trip his only success had been as runner-up in one 14s event to the leading Swedish boy. But he now knew what was required to reach the top, and he worked feverishly before returning to Europe with his mate Hartnett the following year. Cash's determination came shining through during the Avvenire Cup in Milan when the gifted Hartnett was injured while beating Henrik Sundstrom in the singles final. Australia had to win the doubles to beat the Swedish team on points and the demon in Cash carried Hartnett through a torrid match. It confirmed to Barclay that he was potentially one of the best players in the world. 'I remember walking away that night with Jackie and I told her he would win Wimbledon one day,' Barclay said. Cash had turned 15 the previous week.

For Hartnett the ensuing years were fraught with the frustration of injury. He slipped behind Cash after returning to school to complete his Higher School Certificate and never caught up again following a succession of back, shoulder and arm ailments. Hartnett still plays on satellite circuits and continues to wrestle with injury problems. He spent a week with Cash in Düsseldorf during the Nations Cup in May this year, on his way home after suffering another injury. Barclay remains convinced that Cash and Hartnett would have become one of the world's greatest doubles combinations if the left-hander's body had stood the strain. 'Even at 15 they were like old men who had played together for years; they knew every move the other would make. Hartnett had great flair and Cash never missed a return. Mark had the touch and Pat added the power. At times they used to lairise when we were away. They were a couple of devils with the girls, good-looking kids who just seemed to attract attention. They would play shots while looking at a girl and find themselves 3-1 down in the second set. I would walk away

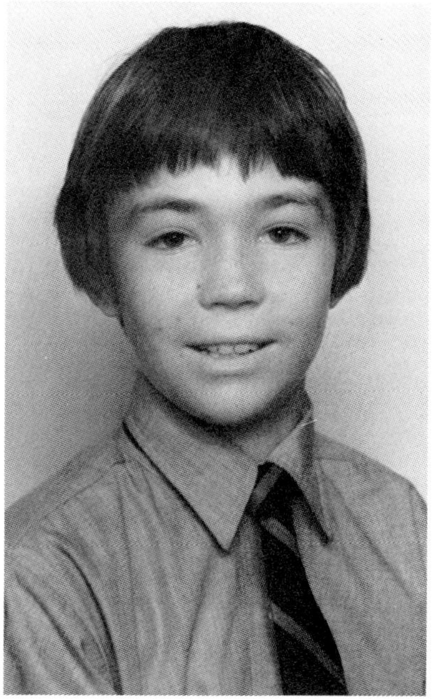

Pat Cash, schoolboy *

muttering in disgust and they would snigger, get stuck into it and demolish the opposition.'

As Cash progressed so did the attention focused on this fiery little fellow's temper. Barclay never doubted his ability to overcome those frustrations with maturity and worked to channel that aggression into productive pursuits on court. From his teenage days Cash was often condemned for his expressive ways. At times it became a fine line between what was a tantrum and merely that inherent desire to win at any cost. 'I knew if I put the fire out, the tennis player in him would die too,' Barclay said. 'When he was inhibited and didn't let off steam, he was hopeless. Once he got it out of his system, he would murder an opponent. It became a matter of harnessing it.' In a post-match press conference at Wimbledon this year, Barclay derived enormous satisfaction from telling the world tennis media: 'We've had tremendous ups and downs and I've been told that whatever happened I would never make a tennis player out of Pat Cash. We received a lot of rubbishing with people saying his temperament would never allow it. We've proved them wrong.' As late as the 1987 Ford Australian Open, some people still wanted to bring down the country's top tennis player. Tennis writers were shocked and appalled to witness a former champion and a veteran scribe gleefully 'celebrating' Cash's demise to Sweden's Stefan Edberg in a fluctuating five-sets final. Either they won't forgive past misdemeanours or can't accept that he has matured from the brash youngster of a few years ago. Gone, it seems, is the scowling young man who once gave the impression of believing every tennis writer was hell-bent on dipping their pens in his blood. Once characterised as a 'diamond in the rough', that competitive spirit has finally won over most of the detractors. A pocket of resistance remains . . . and probably would still spit his surname if he won the Nobel Prize.

Patrick Cash is a forthright fellow, not easy to get to know but fiercely loyal to those he considers as friends. From an early age he was taught to stand up for what he perceived to be his rights. In schooldays that hard-nosed conviction was often mistaken for a bullish attitude, and the more the teachers tried to tame him by intimidation, the harder he fought them. By the time he reached 15 it was obvious the textbooks at Whitefriars College at Donvale in Melbourne's eastern suburbs were the poor relations to a tennis racquet, and his father removed him from the cloistered classroom disciplines and restrictions.

He has retained a close attachment to his father and, significantly, that's who he wanted to reach first when he made the sheepdog dash over spectators to the competitors' box after sweeping aside the world's No. 1, Ivan Lendl, 7-6, 6-2, 7-5 on Wimbledon's centre court. Bjorn Borg sank to his knees in thanksgiving, Jimmy Connors ran to kiss his wife in the second row and Stan Smith vaulted the net after winning their Wimbledons. But, really, to trample over 101 years of Wimbledon tradition and clamber halfway up the stand in full view of the Royal Box! Simply, Cash, the colt they couldn't rope, was driven into the arms of The Clan, the inner circle of family and friends who closed around him in times of tribulation and triumph these past several years. Far from being offended by the wait, the Royal Box occupants delighted in the spontaneous 'ocker' celebration of his victory.

Cash is a daring, tenacious and willing combatant who thrives when the challenge is greatest. He is blessed, some might say burdened, with that wild streak which occasionally plunges him into hot water, but which is so often at the very root of the success. Davis Cup, the demands of representing country instead of self, brings out the best and worst in him. Australian captain Neale Fraser has endured a decade of despair and

delight as he takes the reins from Barclay and attempts to steer Cash on course during each tie. Fraser is another who has ridden Cash's roller-coaster career, at times fiercely protective, occasionally squirming over misdemeanours that ran directly against the grain of his integrity. He admits this remarkable young man has engraved a few more furrows on the brow and, yet, in the next breath, pours out gratitude for providing irreplaceable memories. Since Cash burst into the Australian Davis Cup team to bullock

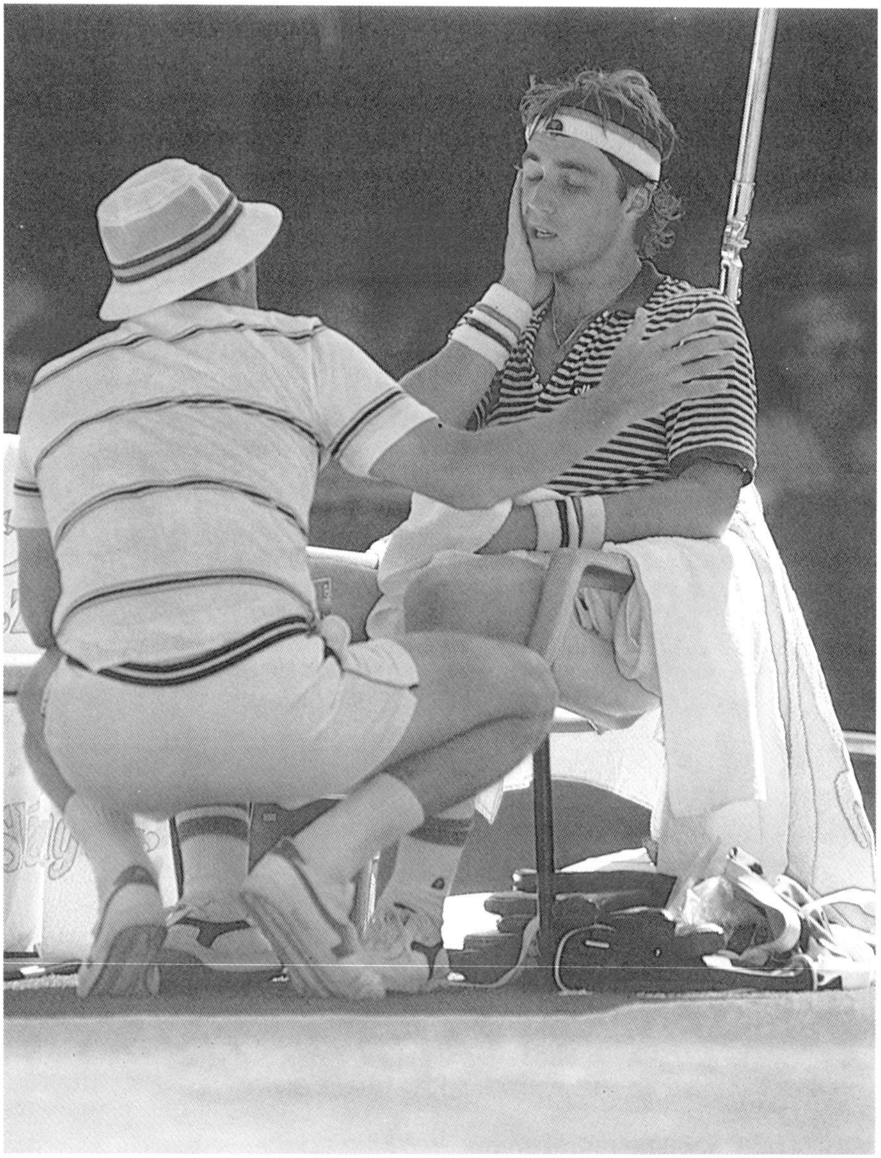

Neale Fraser and Pat Cash. Cash's first Davis Cup, March 1983

aside Briton John Lloyd in a five-sets opening day debut in Adelaide in March 1983, Fraser has, with kid glove, been the director and protector. For the skipper to describe the relationship as having 'gone through our highs and lows' is an understatement akin to describing John McEnroe as a volatile performer.

Still vivid in the mind was the eve of the 1983 Davis Cup final against Sweden at Kooyong when, according to the skipper, he came close to kicking Cash out of the team. Cash disagrees, believing the incident was exaggerated. The local hero and John Fitzgerald, another unrelenting worker, had engaged in their own brand of two-man war after Fraser, in keeping with his normal program, pitted his men in head-to-head combat on centre court in the last days leading up to the tie. Under comical and slightly bizarre circumstances, the lid blew on the pressure-packed scene when a relative of Cash sitting in the near-deserted stand unwittingly became involved in a line-call dispute. In the end a furious and frustrated Cash bounced his racquet which cannoned on to the canvas awning of a courtside private box and was catapulted into the stand. To defuse the centre-court time bomb, Fraser said he sent Cash to the dressing rooms like a chastened schoolboy to cool down. That night the worried captain tossed and turned over whether to gamble on the angry young man who obviously was feeling the strain of the impending duty before the home-town fans. His judgement was stunningly vindicated on the last day when Cash blitzed Swede Joakim Nystrom in straight sets to clinch the final.

Again the team's cornerstone gave Fraser concern two days before the start of the 1986 Cup final at Kooyong. Not surprisingly, it was against Fitzgerald in centre court match-practice that Cash, annoyed at a failed first serve, stormed from the stadium and later clashed with an ABC television crew which ventured too close as he struggled to put a child's pusher in the back of his car. All was forgiven if not forgotten when Cash led from the front to again secure the silver bowl for Australia with a stunning five-sets recovery against a furiously fighting Mikael Pernfors of Sweden. The wave of admiration that washed around the Kooyong stadium after that comeback from a two-sets deficit extended as far as Ted Tinling, that septuagenarian stickler who has little sympathy for the excesses of the younger generation. Tinling purposefully made for Cash as the player came into the interview room and asked: 'May I congratulate you?' That brief and genuine enquiry spoke a thousand words to emphasise that Cash will be remembered by future tennis historians for his indomitable spirit and stroke power rather than isolated outbursts of Irish temper.

No doubt the crippling back injury that removed him from the circuit for the latter half of 1985 and the start of the 1986 tournament calendar

Anne-Britt and Pat

prompted this hard-rock devotee to turn down the volume of his life. Into Cash's seemingly shattered tennis existence sauntered a striking Norwegian-born model Anne-Britt Kristiansen who took a shine to the Aussie following a party thrown by Vitas Gerulaitis in the US. Soon the pair were inseparable – except, of course, for her modelling engagements and his tennis commitments – and she as much as the medical specialists must be credited with helping him overcome the traumas of a herniated disc in the lower back.

So too is a lively little fellow named Daniel Patrick Cash, conceived in love during a holiday in north Queensland and who arrived right on cue on 27 May, 1986, a 21st birthday gift for his proud Dad. In pre-natal days Barclay and Fraser never had trouble tracking down Cash . . . the blast of Iron Maiden or a comparable heavy metal group clearly signalling the music-mad tennis player's whereabouts. These days the electric guitar is as much a part of the luggage as racquets and nappies. But now the music blasts only through headphones and Daniel, rather than the guitar, nestles on the lap. He's unashamedly proud of fatherhood, with a deeper appreciation of the cruel realities of life, no doubt heightened by the injury setbacks.

With the band *

There is a tranquil, air about Cash these days which is as impressive as it is surprising. It first became evident during the opening ceremony of his Davis Cup return in a first-round tie against New Zealand in Auckland in March, 1986. When introduced, he stepped forward, grinning and bowing to the crowd at centre court. It was a friendly, exaggerated gesture straight out of Test cricketer Greg Matthews' manual on crowd-wooing. The Kiwis loved it and the enthusiastic response belied the previously accepted public image of the man. Anne-Britt, Daniel and eight months to ponder the chilling prospect that he might never come back brought a reassessment of his values and attitudes.

His public image continued to take an upturn on his return to tournament tennis, aided by a greater appreciation of the media's job and the value of positive publicity. Cash maintained that previously the media had misled the public in its portrayal of him, and for a time he dreaded the walk to the interview room after a match. Frankly, he felt everyone was against him, a mutual distrust for which both player and press must share the blame. Prior to Cash's comeback from injury, stories abounded in sports-writing circles of confrontations with the Cash family – invective poured on innocent questioners and, of course, the more public displays of petulance which have not gone unrecorded.

Cash is no on-court angel. The make-up of the man is such that he can't produce his best unless he goes for the jugular and such a mentality will

The champion, Wimbledon 1987

US Open junior title 1981

Junior winner US Open 1982

Australian Open 1982

Victorian Open winner 1982

Pat, Anne-Britt and three-week-old Daniel *

inevitably lead to further clashes. He doesn't run and hide from incidents such as the racquet tossed into the crowd after losing a five-sets US Open semi-final to Ivan Lendl in 1984. Nor from the Davis Cup blow-ups. What really makes him mad is when people don't care to hear his explanation. In such an emotionally-charged business, Cash has found a simple way to avoid the head-on confrontations with the often baiting questioners at post-match press conferences. He insists on first taking a shower and a massage to cool down the mind as much as the body before approaching the interview dais. Such a delay annoys those on a deadline, but you can't please everyone.

When he reluctantly agreed to accept a wild card into the main draw at the 1986 Wimbledon championships, he became a 'natural' for the London tabloids. A burly Aussie with longish hair who climbed from his hospital bed and turned up at the All England Club not with, just a diamond stud in his left ear, an appendix scar and a svelte Scandinavian blonde on his right arm, but an infant son as well! The contrasts of Cash the rebel rocker and Cash the proud parent intrigued Fleet Street even more than his splendid exploits to reach the quarter-finals with virtually no preparation.

Now, despite a family-man image, Cash remains a favourite with teenagers around the world who can relate to his questioning rather than blind acceptance of authority. He has required a police escort at the past

US Open 1984

two Wimbledon championships to reach outside courts and sends the girls into a frenzy with the pop-star antics of throwing sweat-stained headbands into the pressing masses after a match. The off-court attention has become easier for him to handle if not accept. Given time, he will stand for as long as possible signing autographs and posing for photographs, with one important proviso . . . so long as it doesn't interfere with practice, training or whatever is required to win the next tennis match.

Typical of the added demands on a Wimbledon champ was Cash's brief refuelling stop in Singapore on the way home after capturing the greatest individual prize in tennis. Wearied by jet lag, Cash lay down in the comparative privacy of the VIP lounge for a nap. No sooner had his head hit the cushion than he was awakened by a woman who supervised this so-called passenger retreat. She had telephoned her son and wanted Cash to explain to the eager youngster how to become a tennis star. 'I drew the line at tennis lessons over the phone in the middle of the night. I was so tired I was like a Zombie,' Cash grinned on his arrival back in Melbourne for a civic reception. 'I'd already signed a stack of autographs for her. Anyway, I would have told him to keep practising.'

A few weeks later Cash was imprisoned in his hotel suite in Brisbane during the Davis Cup quarter-final against Mexico. Without Anne-Britt and Daniel, he sought solace from the strings of his electric guitar and ordered room service for most meals. While teammates Wally Masur, Peter Doohan, John Fitzgerald and Brad Drewett mixed freely with other hotel patrons in the breakfast room, Cash felt compelled to dine alone. He regarded the regimented training and practice schedules as too tight to allow half an hour's wrestling with a bowl of cereal and autograph hunters. Only for team dinners did Cash venture to the restaurants where he could be strategically seated to short-circuit the ill-timed well-wishers.

Increasingly, he will rely on the shield of his loyal entourage, particularly Barclay, to ensure a clear path to the tennis court. Like Boris Becker and Chris Evert Lloyd, the Australian now must insist on a one-in-all-in conference of electronic and print media on arrival for a tournament, otherwise he would spend the first two days talking instead of working. So persistent was the ringing telephone – an unlisted number – at Cash's new five-bedroom abode at Fulham in London's West on the morning of the Wimbledon final that Barclay took the receiver off the hook at 8.30. The Prime Minister Mr Hawke was among the well-meaning followers who couldn't get through to unwittingly place more pressure on the young finalist.

Manfully, Cash carried on his broad shoulders the expectations of a nation ravenous for international tennis success, and rode that powerful serve to glory on the world's most intimidating tennis stage. Already he has made a pilgrimage back to the famed centre court at the All England Club of which he is now a member. A week after the final he returned with close friend Paul McNamee to put the finishing touches to a French-produced television documentary on his life. 'They let me use the centre court for filming. After all, it is my club,' Cash teased, content in the knowledge that honorary membership is bestowed on each singles champion. 'Generally they dig up the courts after the tournament. But the centre was untouched and it was a strange feeling seeing all those familiar marks, the drag marks from my serve. It seemed this was my centre court; I really felt like the owner.'

ellesse

2 Early Days

Imagine a fresh-faced kid at the other end of the tennis court prepared to pin you to the baseline for several minutes merely to win a single point. A 15-year-old who has forgotten more about hustling than the average player would pick up in years of Saturday afternoon social slog. Stalling on the big points, querying line calls, gesturing to his coach and generally dictating the pace of proceedings. A wide-eyed Pat Cash and a group of equally stunned Australians stumbled headlong into this monster of modern tennis on their first overseas trip in 1979.

The initiation to international tournament play came when coach Ian Barclay took his star pupils, Cash, 14, Mark Hartnett, 15, Anne Minter, 16 and Elizabeth Minter, 13, along with a 16-year-old Canberra youth Wally Masur on a privately sponsored European tour to gain experience. For each of them the shock was more than merely the culture. Confronted with opponents who didn't make unforced errors, just kept the ball in play, kept it constantly moving. Back home the Australian group was so dominant that it was considered laborious if a point lasted more than half-a-dozen shots. Suddenly they were forced to acclimatise so drastically that it required hanging on a rally for perhaps 40 or 50 shots merely to win the point. Such a frightening experience on clay is vividly moulded in Cash's mind several years later.

'I still remember when we came back from that trip and Barkers warned that the Czechs and the Swedes were going to be the players of the future. How right can you be!' Cash said. 'We couldn't believe how good these European guys were and that really shook us up a bit. At the time we were all No. 1 in our age groups back home. But the No. 2 guy in our country was

Standing: Mark Hartnett, Pat Cash, Wally Masur. Seated: Elizabeth Minter, Ian Barclay, Anne Minter.*

equivalent to just a better than average player in the same age group overseas. It was the first time away for any of us. All of a sudden – bang – we ran straight into the big guns. We had a limited budget and couldn't afford a few weeks preparation on the clay. Mark won a couple of rounds and the same with Wally who lost to the eventual winner. Me, I was only 14 playing under-16, so I got the tripe beaten out of me,' he said.

What struck the young Australians were the dozens of Bjorn Borg clones . . . right down to his unflustered on-court demeanour. No hustling from the Swedish kids, instead severe topspin off both sides and all double-fisted on the backhand. 'We couldn't believe it. Borg at that stage had won a few of his Wimbledons and all the Swedes were identical to him. Mats Wilander was the first one there and we just said, "that's Borg". Libor Pimek, the Czechoslovakian guy, was there with his double-hander too. All these guys were exactly the same and the Italians played like Adriano Panatta. Sliced backhand, coming over the top, solid all round and never made a mistake.'

The Australians with their shoestring-budget tour were in sharp contrast with the six Swedish junior teams. These each had a coach to conduct the moves from the side of the court and a manager to handle the business details. The Czechs basically kept to themselves: kids from special sporting schools, with their day divided between practice sessions and private academic tuition. With so much government backing for tennis in Europe, Barclay's troupe became an oddity: privately sponsored by the group of businessmen back home.

Barclay remembered returning with mixed feelings – content that the Australian youngsters had at least made the Europeans sit up and take notice, though he was sceptical about the future. Despite the seemingly mediocre results, Cash now knew what he had to do to reach the top. He was eager for work, work and more work with Barclay.

'The first time I heard about Ian Barclay was when I went to school at Whitefriars College. Mark (Hartnett) was at St Kevin's and I found that Warren Brennan was in my class. Mark and Warren used to play in state and national finals all the time and I was playing an age group below. Warren was the only kid I knew at the whole school and he was telling me that there was this really good coach and I should come down,' Cash recalled. It was mutual admiration at that first assessment session, with Barclay quietly reassuring the parents that he liked what he saw and the eager kid just busting to hit with kids bigger and better than himself. 'That was exactly what I wanted because I was hitting the ball all right, but I needed to hit with better people. It's the only way a kid can improve, to hit with players better than you. It was great practice for me and I just improved more and more. After about half the year I went to my first national championships in Sydney.'

Cash lost to Tasmanian Simon Youl, the eventual winner, in the quarter-finals on White City's grass, his first trial on a surface he would eventually conquer like no other player in the world. What Cash remembered more than Youl's sliced backhand and penetrating volleys was the holiday atmosphere of that first trip away. The riotous fun of swimming competitions in the pool at the Brennans' house where the group stayed at Killarney Heights on Sydney's north shore. It was an unforgettable experience, particularly for a lad who, according to his mother, was never keen even to stay overnight at a friend's house and rarely ventured to a school camp.

Losses to Youl and another local player Mark Beers, now a Collingwood footballer, stirred him. Even more significant was being beaten by a younger competitor. 'There was a guy called Ronnie Woodbridge, a year younger than me, who beat me one time in the semi-finals at Donvale Tennis Club. I wasn't too impressed about that because he was younger,' Cash said. Woodbridge, like Hartnett, plays pennant for a Melbourne club and still competes in satellite tournaments in Australia. But it was the breakthrough against his good mate Hartnett which really set the young lion roaring. 'I had practised hard over summer and played tournaments and, when I came back, Mark was still better than me. As soon as I beat Mark,

The young footballer *

that was it; I beat everyone in the juniors clearly. To beat a player such as Mark was an important occasion for me.'

It seemed that every time Barclay turned around, young Cash was there, tugging at the tennis sleeve to hit balls. More and more the pair forged the bonds of friendship and trust, perhaps Barclay was reliving his early tennis years through his patience with the demanding pupil. Barclay, the former youngster who had pushed his way through betting rings at racetracks to run the tote odds, became an A-pennant player with East Malvern at 18. But he bemoaned the lack of tennis interest from his racing-orientated family. Barclay once recalled: 'I think my father only saw me play twice when I was trying to make the grade. Once when I beat Bob Carmichael at St Kilda and the other time I was slaughtered by Roy Emerson in the third round of the Australian championships at Kooyong.' As a tennis coach he bore a crucial characteristic, an understanding of how people, especially the young, were feeling both in a tight match and off the court.

Cash retains absolute faith in his master. 'I have seen a lot of coaches and he's the only one who's basically a specialist. He just seems to know everything about coaching, about juniors. When we went away he knew exactly how we should play. It wasn't as if he was a beginner who couldn't play at all. He played all the guys, the top Australian players and he wasn't good enough to go further. But he knew what was going on, coaching juniors and bringing them along. It just goes to show you don't have to be the best tennis player in the world to coach. Football also proves it.'

Like most Melbourne boys, Cash was raised on a sporting diet liberally sprinkled with the Australian Rules football code. Always bulky for his age, he began bursting through packs in the schoolyard at Our Lady of Good Counsel in Deepdene. Strangely, the little Catholic primary school, with two tennis courts across the road, spawned the last two Australian players to reach the world's top 10. 'It was also Peter McNamara's first tennis club. It's an amazing coincidence. We talk about it sometimes. In recent years I found out during a run near the school with Ann Quinn that she used to go there to get coached too.' Cash started his football with Kew Rovers, a local team coached by former top Australian athlete Tim O'Shannessy. The team utilised Cash's strength by alternating him between the ruck and centre-half-forward. Once he kicked 18 goals from centre-half-forward in a junior match.

With father an ex-footballer, he naturally lived a large slice of childhood clad in the beloved Hawthorn guernsey. One of the vivid memories of his brief yet spectacular football career came on the night he was to be presented with the Under-12s best and fairest award in the Hawthorn District League. Robert Di Pierdomenico, the 1986 Brownlow Medallist, was one of the young players sent by the club to the presentation night. 'We were at the Hawthorn Town Hall and a few of the players came along to say hello to the kids before we went in. It was great thrill. I remember Dipper was there because we could never pronounce his name.' Whenever Cash is home during winter, he always tries to get to a Hawthorn match and chat with the players in the dressing rooms later. Di Pierdomenico and Cash, both with unique styles, retain mutual admiration for their sporting feats. 'I must tell Dipper about that presentation night,' Cash grinned.

Bologna 1980 *

Whether it was cricket in summer, football in winter or tennis every other waking hour, Cash tackled it with a burning competitive spirit. That strive for perfection was poignantly illustrated during a junior football final at the Glenferrie Oval one day. 'I only kicked two goals for the match and I was so mad,' Cash remembered. 'Even though we had won the semi-final, I was in a filthy mood because I didn't kick more goals. It says something about my tennis too. Even if I have won but played badly I'm still not happy. I would be happier playing great and losing to someone who has played better.'

Increasingly, tennis and football proved a difficult marriage. Both the pennant tennis and junior football competitions were played on Sunday afternoon and young Cash valiantly attempted to fulfil commitments. 'At that stage my tennis had improved to the point where I was top in my age group and I had the chance to play C-special pennant. To play against men seemed to be bigger than junior football. I remember Barkers telling me that the first pennant match was always the toughest and I was so bloody nervous thinking about it. I went out and beat this guy 7-5, 6-4 which should have been 2 and 2. I was so keyed up, believing that if you get through the first one then you are right. If he hadn't said anything I probably would have killed the guy.'

Bari 1980 *

When Cash's football club was promoted to the Doncaster League, he was keen to help out by playing matches against stronger teams. Strangely, his football memories are clearest, not with playing highlights, but rather on significant incidents. Like the time he committed a blatant infringement to the rules and another match when he KO'd one of his best mates, Dean Barclay, the son of the coach.

'I was playing in the ruck against Macleod who had this guy who seemed to be 6'5". I was able to jump and I kind of did a Don Scott by running straight at him. I was doing okay but he was so tall that he just stuck his arms up whenever the ball came down. The ball came down and I pushed the guy in the back, took the mark and turned around and ran 10 metres to kick the goal. That was the first time I ever did anything illegal on purpose in footy. I pushed this guy in the back and got away with it. It was a really weird feeling. I will never forget that.'

No doubt, his mate Dean can't remember portions of a particular final he played for Heatherdale Football Club against Cash's team. Cash had to play a pennant match at Grace Park in Hawthorn and then dash to the football at Xavier College, only a couple of kilometres away. 'I played the pennant match against a kid who was my age and beat him 6-1, 6-1 in about two hours. This kid wouldn't miss and, instead of taking half-an-hour, it took two hours.' By the time Cash arrived at the football it was three-quarter-time and the coach decided to throw him into the fray. 'It was the first time I had ever come on as a reserve and I was getting so frustrated trying to get into the play. All the opposition players were giving me heaps because they were winning, telling me I was too scared to play the whole match. I was getting madder and madder and finally I just went, bang, sunk my boot into a pack trying to kick the ball.' Unfortunately, he missed the leather and cleaned up the hapless and innocent Dean.

Gradually, as the trips overseas to junior tennis events ate more into the winter sporting timetable, Cash's football interest became confined to watching Hawthorn play on a Saturday afternoon with Dean. And the Carmelite Fathers at Whitefriars College weren't exactly tuning into Radio Milan to catch the latest match results of their wandering fourth-year student. So devastated was the 15-year-old's academic year by tennis commitments that he sat examinations in only two subjects. Frankly, tennis six days a week and a two-month overseas tour mid-year didn't leave much study time for a boy who admitted that he wasn't particularly dedicated to school work. He had an ambition then 'to win a few million', a prospect infinitely more appetising to a teenager than Shakespeare and Isaac Newton. At 15, he had already become the youngest player to win the Victorian hardcourt singles title and, with a degree of trepidation, his parents

Doubles final, Avvenire Cup, Milan 1980. Cash and Hartnett (far court) v Benhabiles and Corteau. Barclay: 'I remember walking away that night with Jackie and I told her Pat would win Wimbledon one day.'*

permanently removed their boy from the classroom. It was a decision not taken lightly by the family. Not only did Pat leave school, but home as well. At 15 he spent seven months away, either on tour or training at the Sports Institute in Canberra.

To this day Cash hasn't returned to his old school . . . and, really, has no intentions in the immediate future. The constant hassles with the staff are embedded in the mind. 'I have never really wanted to go back to Whitefriars, I have bitter memories of it. For about five years after I left I hated school teachers. Anybody that was a school teacher, I wouldn't talk to them. I'm serious. I looked at them in a low light, they thought they were better than the kids and treated them like dirt. Gradually I have got to meet a few, mainly girls, teaching at primary school and older guys such as headmasters. I know now they are normal people trying to do a job. But when I was at school they were like cops to me.' Cash shuddered at the thought of his younger brother Daniel following him to college. Like big brother, Daniel was rebellious, but quieter, and his joking nature defused many potential confrontations.

Not surprisingly, Cash related best to sports teachers – former Fitzroy Football Club captain Garry Wilson and the senior team's runner and fitness adviser Ray Keane. In particular he retained a grudging respect for the gregarious Keane with his sergeant-major voice and commanding ways. There wasn't a Fitzroy footballer of the late 70s and early 80s who hadn't felt the sting of Keane's matter-of-fact tone and, more than once, Cash endured a blast from the sports master at Whitefriars. Cash recalled one clash on the school's sports oval during his last year as his ears burned from the full blast of Keane's booming voice. 'As I walked off I said, "you're just the same as all of them" and he snapped that he wanted to see me later. I remember going into his office and, after warning me of the punishments such as detention, he said, "all I want you to know is that I'm not like the other teachers and you know it!" He was right and I apologised. He was a good guy and I felt closer to him than anyone. I got on really well with Garry (Wilson) who was much quieter. Ray was bossier, he's now the head sports teacher at another school and actually I want to go back and say hello to him.'

Freed from the shackles of schoolbooks, the young man could vent his spleen on a tennis ball in practice with Barclay. His world junior ranking rose dramatically in 1981, an important year with such a radical change of direction in his tennis life. Cash spent part of the year at the tennis sector of the Australian Institute of Sport in Canberra. There he was under the control of national coach Ray Ruffels, a very dedicated and wily wielder of a racquet. He was the ideal man to take a team of youngsters around the

The Avvenire Cup *

Stefan Edberg and Pat Cash: the Avvenire Cup win *

world. He had pulled every trick in the book and a few more in his years wandering the international circuit, winning tournaments and representing his country in Davis Cup during an era when Australian players were admired as much for their beer-drinking and partying as their no-nonsense approach on court. Social attitudes had relaxed since the days when the late Harry Hopman ruled Australian teams with unquestioned discipline. Nevertheless, the cadre spirit remained as Ruffels led an Australian junior team on tour. Cash was pursued by girls and agents in his first full year on the circuit as he won titles in Bari and Milan before the troupe reached the English grass courts. To win the elite Avvenire Cup in Milan, he had to beat Emilio Sanchez of Spain in the quarters, Karel Novacek of Czechosolvakia in the semis and Stefan Edberg of Sweden in the final.

He then began his love affair with the manicured turf at the All England Club, but after reaching the Wimbledon boys singles final was beaten 7-6, 7-5 by American Mat Anger. For the first time Cash felt weighed down by the expectations to succeed. A telegram from a close relative on the eve of the final gave an already knotted stomach an extra twist as he walked out to face Anger.

What hit home to Cash as he eased into senior ranks was the need to smarten his attitude to physical work, particularly away from the court. His muscular build was such that he never required weight work to develop strength and, basically, relied on natural ability and brute power to subdue his junior foes. 'I was basically lazy when I went to the Institute. I never wanted to go for a run, I hated running. I could play tennis all day but I was lazy. I used to get fit simply by playing tennis until I started to practise with the Davis Cup team and realised how hard they worked. It wasn't until after I had my bad back that I really learned how the body worked.'

At 16, on returning from overseas, he always headed straight for Barclay. 'We were still putting Pat's game together. He didn't become a competent serve-volleyer until 16,' Barclay recalled. One winter day in 1981, Cash was hitting with the coach at a court in a Ringwood park when Chris Gleeson, managing director of Australian Diagnostics Corporation stopped his car to watch. As a friend of Barclay, he enquired on the boy's progress and found he wanted to improve his junior ranking by playing the Canadian and US championships. Gleeson provided the air fare and the plan was for Cash to stay with an Australian who ran a tennis camp on the US east coast. When Cash finally rang home the family pieced together a jumbled tale from the trans-Pacific phone conversation. Young Cash, obviously looking bewildered at bustling Kennedy Airport in New York, was befriended by a woman who eventually took him home for a couple of days. Cash's only concern was that she shrank his tennis shirts in the wash.

Amid the 'little boy lost' turmoil, Cash won the Canadian juniors and lost to West German Hans Schwaier in the US semi-finals. By virtue of sound performance in the Grand Slam boys singles events – he lost to Mats Wilander in the French quarters, reached the Wimbledon final and US semis and lost the Australian final to Sweden's Jorgen Windahl – Cash was voted the International Tennis Federation No. 1 junior that year.

The small crowd that sat into the early hours one morning at the Frankston indoor tennis centre witnessed Cash's arrival in senior ranks by beating Syd Ball of NSW 6-0, 6-2 in a 65 minutes first-round match. Ball, 14 years the senior, was helpless against the relentless if raw Cash power. Inevitably the youngster fell next round to top seed Vitas Gerulaitis, who shocked the tennis family to its back teeth by forfeiting to local hero Peter McNamara midway through the final as the ultimate protest over bad line calls.

Now the heat was really turned on Cash, particularly the comparison with Wilander who won the 1982 French Open crown at 17, and made the fourth round at Wimbledon when the Australian failed to qualify for the men's singles draw in either championship. Still, those closely watching Cash's progress were not restless and permitted themselves a satisfied nod after Cash won the Wimbledon boys singles title, beating Henrik Sundstrom of Sweden 6-4, 6-7, 7-5 in the final. On the way he beat Jakob Hlasek, Tarik Benhabiles and Loic Courteau. And he recovered from a service breakdown in the third set against Sundstrom. 'If Pat is prepared to pay the price, he can go all the way,' was Ruffels' prophetic summary. Cash senior recalled venturing to the Wimbledon dressing rooms to give his son a congratulatory hug. The weary victor looked up and said: 'I've won the little one, Dad. Now I'm going after the big one.'

The Wimbledon boys' singles title *

3 Davis Cup

Pat's first Davis Cup match

Triumphant Americas' Cup skipper John Bertrand went into a huddle with Pat Cash deep in the concrete bowels of the old Kooyong stadium. His imminent tennis task was similar to Bertrand's, when he had headed out for that last race on the waters off Newport. Forget the past, what matters is the job at hand . . . and that's to win. In less than two hours Cash, at 18 the baby of Australia's Davis Cup team, fanned the flames of nationalistic fervor again to bring another silver trophy Down Under. Cash rekindled memories of Hoad and Rosewall, blasting Swede Joakim Nystrom off the worn centre court grass 6-4, 6-1, 6-1 to secure an unassailable 3-1 lead in the 1983 Davis Cup final.

Four battling Australian tennis players, inspired by a yacht and its skipper, had defied the odds to bring back the Davis Cup. At the request of captain Neale Fraser, Australia II skipper Bertrand came to the dressing room before and after each match of the final against the higher-ranked Sweden team to keep pumping the adrenalin and national pride. Cash, John Fitzgerald, Paul McNamee and Mark Edmondson were still riding the wave of achievement that broke in their Sydney hotel rooms during the semi-final against France in September after watching Australia II glide to the gun to beat Liberty 4-3 off the US east coast.

To be frank, Cash wasn't carried away by the chest-thumping, green and gold flag bearers. Like so many individual sportsmen and sportswomen, he prefers to be left alone, even by coach and family, immediately prior to a match. But he conceded that he had committed to mind the lesson of the Americas' Cup last race before walking into Melbourne's December sunshine to play Nystrom. Cash recalled: 'Frase thought it would be a good idea to have Bertrand in the rooms. To be honest, I didn't like the idea of outsiders because we wanted to concentrate on the match. Don't get me wrong, it was great to have John's support there. But there's the Prime Minister coming in to wish you good luck and then John Bertrand trying to make a speech to you. It's just things you don't need; you are trying to concentrate on the match and get your mind in tune with what's about to happen. What did strike me was one piece of advice, like before that final race in the America's Cup. Instead of thinking of what was going to happen if I lost, I had to focus on winning. You don't want to think negatively, you must think about winning. It was something I had tried to do for those past two days and basically he reiterated exactly what I was thinking.'

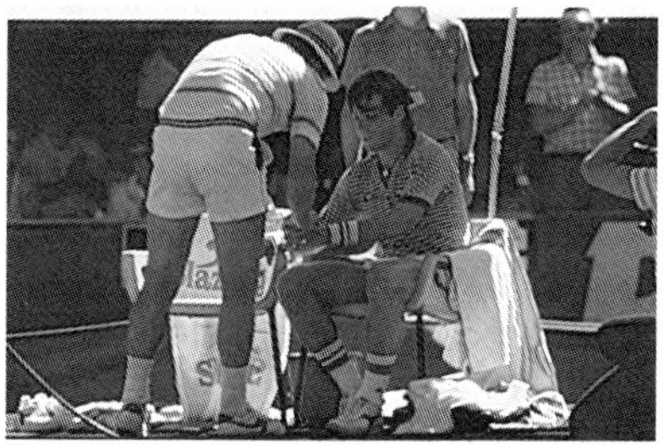

Davis Cup tie against Great Britain, 1983

In only his second year on the circuit, Cash became the youngest player to win the deciding match on the final day of a Davis Cup final, bringing memories of the great Ken Rosewall on the same centre court 30 years earlier. Rosewall, then 19, clinched the Cup for Australia at Kooyong in 1953 with a four-sets win against American Vic Seixas – ironically the referee for the 1983 final. And Cash's victory was the most convincing by an Australian in a final since Roy Emerson demolished Spain's Manuel Santana by the same score in the 1967 Challenge Round in Brisbane. Cash's timely answer to his country's call was emphasised by Swedish ace Mats Wilander, who proved just how close the tie had been by ending Fitzgerald's unbeaten Davis cup record 6-8, 6-0, 6-1 in the last match to reduce the final scoreline to 3-2.

All this achieved by one so young . . . and so aggressive that it nearly cost him a place as Australian singles representative. Fraser revealed the chilling prospect afterwards that he considered discarding Cash because of his attitude to training. Watching Australia's practice sessions leading to the tie was like sitting on the rim of a volcano. Eventually the tension erupted with Cash and Fitzgerald locked in a match practice workout on centre court two days before the official draw. A dispute arose over a line call, Cash bounced his racquet which flew into the stand and Fraser halted play, sending him to the dressing room to cool down.

Fraser said after the tie that he had reprimanded Cash for disruptive practice and told him to cool off in the dressing room. 'I went home that night and thought that we couldn't have Cash in the team. I wasn't happy with his form, it appeared to me he was unhappy with things other than his tennis. He wasn't contributing in the interests of the team and I told him accordingly. But after I spoke to him, his practice session the next day was completely different.'

Cash disputed the notion that he nearly lost his place and described the incident with Fitzgerald as merely part of the healthy, competitive build up to a Davis Cup tie. 'The tension is greater than a tournament as it centres on a few players instead of, say, at Wimbledon where it is spread over 128 players. I bounced my racquet towards my bag and somehow it just kept cartwheeling. At the time it was quite funny. It was the end of the set and I wasn't too happy because I had lost the set or the game before we stopped. It does cheese me off that people believe Frase sent me off the court. That incident was just another and, if you had been there for practice every day, you would have seen worse incidents than that. Practice is when you have to get your steam out somehow.'

Cash explained how tension mounts when Fraser pits his players in head-to-head, game-for-game 'real thing' workouts just before the official draw to gauge which players are the sharpest, the best prepared. 'That is why Australian teams do so well, regardless of rankings. When you are fighting for a singles spot, it is the closest you can get to an actual Davis Cup match. It is simulated because of the enormous pressure and by the time the guy gets through he has played under pressure situations with sets. The competition was so fierce in '83 because any of us could have played.'

It would be unfair to single out Cash for a tempestuous approach to the final as the angry antics of the other team members even prompted the concerned Fraser to summon help from a sports psychologist Laurie Hayden. 'Frase was worried that the practice sessions were getting a bit fierce and he brought us in one morning to have a chat. He [Hayden] was saying to just enjoy it a bit more, look at your good shot and don't be so negative. You don't need to throw or bounce your racquet or swear, just think towards the next point. I remember that about half-an-hour after we started again, racquets were flying everywhere. It was no different at all. Everyone was so intense and we were not used to someone coming in to make a speech. What I have found in my career is that the more normal it is, the better. Anything out of the ordinary is going to make it weird for you.'

More unsavoury than the petulance in practice sessions was the blow-up between three times Wimbledon champion John Newcombe and Cash, or, more correctly, the Cash family, the week prior to the final. The Cashs are not likely to forgive Newcombe for a newspaper article under his name with 'ghost' writer John Thirsk. In short Newcombe said that comparing Mats Wilander and Pat Cash was like comparing the Grand Canyon to a crack in the wall. Certainly, Sweden was favorite to win the Davis Cup final since Wilander had won the Australian Open on the Kooyong grass three weeks previously and then Nystrom captured the NSW Open, beating Cash in the semi-finals. But such an inflammatory statement on the eve of a young Australian's Davis Cup final debut was, to say the least, untimely. Every member of the Cash clan can recite the words by heart although, at the time,

Davis Cup Final against Sweden 1983

Davis Cup semi-final 1986

First round Davis Cup 1987

First round Davis Cup 1987

Davis Cup 1986

Davis Cup team 1986

Australian Open 1987
steel-wristed low forehand volley

Barbeque at Neale Fraser's house to celebrate the Davis Cup win, January 1987. Pat Cash had just had an exploratory knee operation.

they attempted to keep Pat isolated from the furore which erupted from that ill-timed prose. The Cash family felt that such was Newcombe's involvement as a head of the Custom Credit Operation Tennis Scheme that he had an obligation to support Australia's junior players.

'It was just after McEnroe was carrying on and I was starting to get branded like McEnroe and I was feeling it a bit. I don't think I have changed that much from the first time I went on a tennis court in the way I get mad at myself. I'm a perfectionist. I want to hit a winner off every point and now the difference is I am starting to realise it is impractical and I am going to lose a lot of points. I remember someone telling me after the NSW Open semi that Thirsk was clapping for Nystrom to beat me. Then in the press conference he asked why I thought a lot of people had been against me and wanting Nystrom to win. I just answered that he was a good player and a Swede and I didn't make anything of it. But I think people were going off me because of the unwarranted reputation I was gathering, particularly in the Sydney papers, which was a bit unfair. Then when Newcombe canned me before the Davis Cup final, that made it even worse. Basically he was saying that I wasn't the sort of person he wanted playing Davis Cup and we don't want you to win. That's the way I interpreted it and that wasn't a good feeling. I hope someone has kept the article because I would like to look back at it. At the time I knew something was wrong, just the way people were reacting. I wasn't picking up a paper at all. I was scared to read any papers. It's a terrible feeling to pick up the back page and expect something bad is going to be written about you.'

While the barbs dug deep it was the Newcombe-style public admonishment which so often produced the 'us-against-them' philosophy that feeds his intensely competitive nature. Fraser had called up Cash to give him the feel of Davis Cup competition as a squad member to hit and fox balls for John Alexander, Peter McNamara, Paul McNamee, Mark Edmondson and Brad Drewett before the 1982 semi-final against the US in Perth. At the time Fraser remarked that young Cash was the fastest Australian player since Roy Emerson. So, with McNamara unavailable for the 1983 first round and Alexander at the end of a grand career, the skipper gambled on the Melbourne youngster who had broken through for his first Grand Prix singles title two months earlier.

With the luck of the Irish and a cool approach to crisis, Cash overcame a 'wrong' racquet and experienced Englishman John Lloyd in a heart-wrenching Davis Cup debut in Adelaide in March, 1983. Lloyd held a service break in the fifth set and was within a point of a double break to bring Cash to his knees on the Memorial Drive turf. A lucky shoot off the frame which landed on the line provided breathing space and Cash, too young to vote in the Federal elections that day, served his country instead with a gutsy 5-7, 7-5, 6-3, 1-6, 7-5 victory in four hours. He had got through the stress of a match postponed 24 hours by rain to become the youngest Australian Davis Cup singles player since the late Viv McGrath in the 1930s. Alexander had also been 17 years old when he tackled the American might in doubles in the same city in 1968.

'I had won the Victorian Open a couple of months before and I knew Frase wanted to whack me in. I was trying a mid-sized racquet for the first time but I only had one that I really liked. They sent some of the Vilas wood racquets from England and they were like lead. They were so heavy and I was serving unbelievably well. I was pretty nervous as Lloyd was a tough grass court player and I think he was playing better at the end of his career than at any other stage. I was down a break in the fifth set and I didn't want it to slip away because I was a better player than the guy and I was just missing out all the time. It's a real buzz to win any tight match, but being the first Davis Cup match made it an even bigger thrill.'

Uncle Brian was nearly as tired as his nephew after that weekend sitting in the stand with a jumpy brother, Pat senior. Anyone who has watched Cash senior when his son is playing can testify to the nervy body twitch each time junior strikes the tennis ball. Young Pat had talked him into giving up smoking at that time and father required a stiff drink as well as chewing gum to endure the mental torture of a Cash Davis Cup debut. Brian Cash, also a lawyer, brought back a double brandy.

Following that shaky opening Fraser guided his new young star through a 5-0 quarter-final whitewash of Rumania in Brisbane when Cash conceded only 10 games in five sets against Florin Segarceanu and a past-his-prime Ilie Nastase. On to Sydney for the semi-final against France, Cash lost the opening rubber to Yannick Noah before an apathetic crowd which John Fitzgerald finally coaxed into voice during the next match against Henri Leconte. No-one can dispute it was Fitzy's tie as he beat Noah and Leconte to send Australia through to the final before Cash found touch in the 'dead' rubber against the flashy Leconte.

Directing Cash, 18, and Fitzgerald, 22, became a total contrast of emotions for Fraser. While Fitzgerald fuelled the inner fire by sharing his pumped-up feelings with the crowd and the captain at the change of ends, Cash preferred a quieter, more personal approach. 'It was a totally new experience having Frase there beside the court. He doesn't direct me an awful lot, only if I ask him something will he really say anything and that's the way I like it. If I'm having trouble I'll ask and he will give a suggestion. But unless I'm in deep trouble, he just throws in the odd suggestion. He doesn't tell you exactly where to serve or anything like that and instead

Davis Cup 1983

Victory leap (Photo: *Melbourne Herald*)

might make a comment about the style of the other player. Basically, he leaves it up to the player and I think that's the way to do it. He's always there with reassurance.'

On the opening day of the final, nothing Fraser advised could stop the imperturbable Mats Wilander from beating an emotionally-charged Cash 6-

3, 4-6, 9-7, 6-3 before Fitzgerald squared the tie, downing Joakim Nystrom 6-4, 6-2, 4-6, 6-4. Then Paul McNamee and Mark Edmondson combined brilliantly to beat Anders Jarryd and Hans Simonsson 6-4, 6-4, 6-2 in the critical doubles match. 'I remember Macca was really disappointed at missing a singles spot and, being such a patriotic fellow, he really wanted to show he could do the job. The great quality of Macca is that he came out and played one of the best doubles matches of his life, the day after being bitterly upset at not being selected for singles.'

And so a young man who had just qualified for a licence to drive away from Kooyong had the task of finishing off the Swedes on the final day. The loss to Wilander tuned him for the greatest challenge of his short tennis life. 'We were all serve-volley players and of course we were playing guys who stayed back. Looking back on it now, I wish we had a bit more practice working from the baseline. But Frase kept putting us against each other because he didn't know who to pick and, naturally, we all tried to serve and volley in practice. Even though I was playing well I lost a tight four setter to Wilander.

'On the last day I knew Fitzy had his work cut out to beat Wilander who was the Australian Open champion and I knew this was my chance. I went to bed a couple of hours early to get my ten hours and, sure enough, I was thinking of the Nystrom match for the first two hours. Next morning I was so nervous I couldn't eat. I forced down a bowl of cereal and a piece of toast before I went out to practice. When I walked on to the centre court the first thing that struck me was the pace compared to the outside courts used for practice. It was so fast I hit the first two balls into the fence. I thought, great, this is perfect for me. I was full of confidence and I knew he was staying back. The practice I should have got a couple of days earlier came during the Wilander match. Anyway I got it for Nystrom and felt very comfortable.'

The fall of the names at the official draw had neutralised the dangerous Wilander as he suffered the frustration of sitting in the stand waiting to see if he would be required for combat in the last rubber. Cash showed the gentle Swedes no mercy with remarkably mature and controlled aggression in contrast to the mind-snapping antics in the practice sessions. The well-mannered, baseline-raised Nystrom could not compete with the net-storming pressure applied by the Australian. In the circumstances it was like putting a North Sea salmon in a tank with a killer shark. He could not defend himself. On match point Cash flipped a lob which cannoned off the frame of Nystrom's outstretched racquet and flew harmlessly out of court. Kooyong trembled on its old concrete foundations to the collective roar. The jubilant Cash leapt to punch the sky with a raised right fist and fell into Fraser's arms.

Davis Cup final 1983 – Neale Fraser and Pat Cash

'Frase had to tell me to go and shake hands with Joakim, I just completely lost myself I was so excited. It was a dream come true. Out of nothing I was in the winning Davis Cup team. I don't take any credit for being the last player out there to hit the last ball. Any one of the four of us in the team could have gone out there that day and won the match.'

The Australians had belied the international computer on the big occasion with Wilander, Nystrom and Jarryd ranked ahead of McNamee at 31, Fitzgerald 34, Cash 37 and Edmondson 40. And Cash, who had stormed from the stadium a couple of days earlier, was this time carried to the exit on the emotion of a standing ovation.

The Australians again were the unheralded underdogs with no real ranking pedigrees to suggest greatness in the 1986 international teams competition. Cash and McNamee both were wrestling with comeback problems for the first round against New Zealand in Auckland. Cash rejoined the team lacking match toughness, following the long lay-off with the back injury. His contribution was to partner Fitzgerald in the doubles as the veteran Peter McNamara steered Australia to a 4-1 win with superb displays against Chris Lewis and Kelly Evernden. By the time the Aussies faced another away tie against Britain in late July, Cash had his punishing serve-volley game right back in its groove. He smashed aside Jeremy Bates and Andrew Castle on Wimbledon's No. 1 court for another 4-1 victory to set up a semi-final against the better-credentialled Americans in Brisbane. Again he was the mainstay of the team, sinking Tim Mayotte, ranked 12th in the world, and Brad Gilbert 15th, with ease, despite dropping the opening set of each match.

At the ripe old age of 21, Cash again carried the expectations of a tennis nation. While most young men of comparable age were agonising over their first car or leaving home to join the flat dwellers, he was at the front preparing to face the awesome Swedish tennis army. Despite Mats Wilander's absence, the Scandinavians had the big-serving Stefan Edberg who had swept all before him on Kooyong's centre court 12 months earlier to win the Australian singles title. Edberg, ranked fourth in the world, was backed by Joakim Nystrom 7th, Mikael Pernfors 11th and Anders Jarryd 19th, while Cash, McNamee, Fitzgerald and McNamara stood 24th, 45th 101st and 307th respectively in world singles. 'I felt I had to perform well for us to have a chance of winning. I prepared well, a whole month, and the closer it got the more tense everyone became. Everyone felt the pressure, Barkers included. Anne-Britt and I were getting on each other's nerves and the guys were getting intense. It just built up and up.' Cash was so determined to be totally prepared for the Cup final that he declined a $50,000 offer to play the Young Masters, instead spending five hours a day in Melbourne practising on the grass and working on fitness with Quinn.

A chance airport meeting with Melbourne sports medicine doctor George Jenko had introduced Cash to relaxation via psychology. 'I started to talk to him which is not like me. I like to be by myself when I'm travelling alone. My father had tried to make me look into psychology before, but I thought it was only for someone who had a problem and I didn't want him [Jenko] to think I was a nut-case. He introduced me to relaxation during the semi-final in Brisbane and then I wanted to continue it. George was doing it part-time so I thought I would get a full-time professional. I had started work with Jeff Bond before the final and that saved my sanity a bit, although I was still a bundle of nerves. I was just starting to get my ranking back and I could see the final as the chance for extra confidence and to relive the 1983 dream.'

Despite the psychological defences, the pressure lid blew once again when Fraser threw his high-charged men into that familiar simulated matches routine in the countdown to the official Davis Cup draw. Cash cut short a workout with Fitzgerald in frustration when his fired-up teammate had taken a set and was leading in the second. After becoming increasingly annoyed and frustrated, Cash served a double fault and walked from the court. He bundled up his gear and told Fitzgerald 'I'm bagging it for the day, well played' and stalked from the stadium. An ABC cameraman, taking close-up shots of Cash packing a child's stroller into a car, claimed Cash struck him in the face after telling him to go away. Cash also had words with another television crew near the dressing room entrance, forcefully telling them to leave him alone.

Following the incidents, a barefooted McNamee emerged from the dressing room to act as peacemaker and reassure everyone that the team spirit was intact. 'No-one could try harder for the team than Pat. He has been in such good form but he just went off the boil today and was frustrated', McNamee told the large media contingent. Cash had broken two racquets before the eruption, although it needs to be said that even the mild-mannered Swedes had done their fair share of racquet-hurling during the week.

Cash denied striking the pestering photographer and said he pushed the camera aside after asking three times to be left alone. 'The photographer thing was another bit of the tension building up. I hadn't played very well against Fitzy. In fact it was horrendous and, as a perfectionist, I felt I should have played better. So I wasn't in a good mood. The guy was in the wrong place at the wrong time. I knew I had done something wrong, but I wasn't mad at myself for what I'd done. I knew it was the wrong thing, but I got the frustration out. I'm a bit hot-tempered, that's just the way I am and I know I shouldn't have done it.'

So besieged did Cash feel with the media attention that he walked straight back in to the centre stadium and asked his captain to relieve the burden by leaving him out of the team. The experienced Fraser, who later admitted he could sense the players' moods simmering to the boil, calmed down his agitated young star as the pair stood courtside watching a doubles workout hastily arranged to provide Fitzgerald with further practice following the Cash walk-off. 'It just got too much and I told Frase that I didn't want to play. I didn't want to go out there because there was so much pressure. The feeling of expectation on me and the negative thoughts were coming in. It's terrible to feel nervous like that. You feel negative, then you feel good, you feel positive, then you shake like a leaf. Everything was just muddled up in my brain.'

Amid the post-practice furore Brian Cash, a Rumpole rogue with an impish grin, even made a jocular attempt to temper the indignation surrounding the shocked television cameraman who nearly ended with an eye on a fist instead of the lens. With tongue firmly embedded in cheek, the legal joker sauntered to the concerned media group encircling the outraged cameraman and said: 'If you need a good lawyer, I'm available'. Those who knew him laughed, those who didn't marvelled at the swiftness of his appearance, as slick as a tow-truck to a motor accident.

Cash had his mind and strokes back together by next day as a battery of cameras monitored his every move. It was McNamee's turn to become intoxicated on the pre-battle fumes as he smashed two racquets in a centre stadium performance totally foreign to his usual training demeanor. Cash was back in the groove but still felt threatened by the huge media attention focused on the final's preparations, as if everyone was after his skin. 'After Macca smashed a couple of racquets and Fitzy broke one in practice, Peter McFarline wrote an article in *The Sun* about bad sportmanship. That was a shocker. It came to mind "I'm playing my guts out for you, you bastard". That was my attitude, I'm playing for my country and yet there are people out there who want me to lose, want me to screw up and want to make it even more difficult for me. Even Dad's cousin Peter Cash came up to me the next day before I went out on centre court for practice and told me to take it easy. He said he had overheard a photographer from *The Herald* saying "where's Pat Cash and what's he wearing today? I don't really know what he looks like, but I have to take a photo of him looking angry". I didn't feel comfortable out there on the court with everybody watching me. I'm a tennis player, I'm not a movie star. I never pretend to be something I'm not and just try to hit the ball as well as I can. It's a weird feeling to have people looking at you all the time and for a couple of years people are just looking for me to do something. I can't pick my nose otherwise it might be on the front cover!'

With the unpleasantries of practice behind him, Cash set the fuse to fire Australia away to a confidence-boosting lead in the opening match against the daunting Edberg. After a jittery start which plunged him to a 1-5 deficit, Cash went for the Swede with all the springed energy of a greyhound after a hare. As the Australian buried overheads and volleys into the turf, Edberg's head began to noticeably droop and the shoulders sagged, not from weariness but more the self-doubt of whether he could hold off the tenacious Australian any longer. It took Cash 3 hours 45 minutes to finally subdue the gallant Edberg 13-11, 13-11, 6-4. Like a heavyweight boxer, Cash strode triumphant from the stadium with a raised fist acknowledging the adoring applause from the capacity 12,000 fans. And less than two hours later, a crestfallen McNamee headed for the same exit with a ready-made nightmare on which to toss and turn that night. Pernfors responded to the cheering of a surprisingly large Swedish support group in the sun-drenched stands to whip McNamee 6-3, 6-1, 6-3.

'Before the tie we had reckoned we could afford to lose to Edberg but we had to win the doubles. I'd never figured that Pernfors would play the way he did. It shook us all up. We couldn't believe the way he played on the first day. Paul just felt uncomfortable against him. I wasn't particularly worried, I didn't think he could come out and blast me away like Paul because I was a different player altogether.'

How wrong could he be! When Cash and Fitzgerald perfectly knitted their respective strong serve and blistering returns to blast aside Edberg and Jarryd 6-3, 6-4, 4-6, 6-1 in the doubles, most expected the tie would be over in time for the family to turn off the telly and take the traditional Sunday afternoon outing. Instead little Pernfors, who earlier had a Swedish flag sprayed on his crewcut, chased Cash around the centre court like a terrier snapping at the heels. With a mixture of delicate dinks and doublehanded lobs, Pernfors was determined to take the tie right down to the wire.

So dominant was the scurrying Swede that, after losing the second set, a bewildered Cash turned to McNamara, Fitzgerald and Mark Kratzmann sitting in the front row and called for help. 'I didn't think he would keep it up, I thought it would be for a couple of games and then he would slow down. When I lost the second set I turned to the guys and said "I can't beat this guy, he's playing too good". Deep down I knew I could, I was just trying to get rid of the frustration.'

Somehow Cash maintained composure and gradually he became the centre court predator, hunting down the cocky little Swede. He put the psychology lessons to use by imagining the centre court was surrounded by glass to lock out the deafening roars as the Australian and Swedish cheer squads set up a cacophony of chants through the entire 3 hour 30 minute

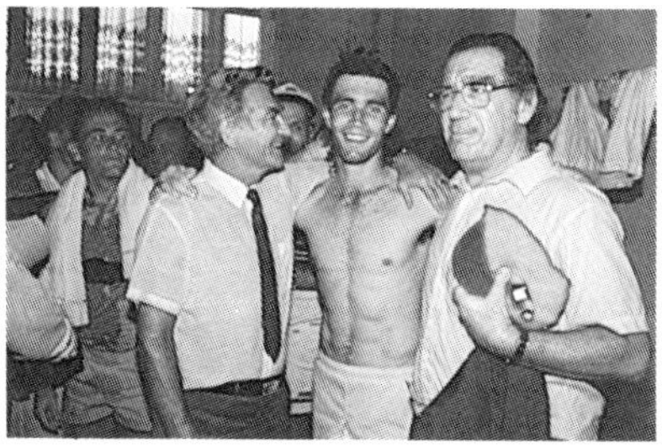

Mikael Pernfors, Bob Hawke, Pat Cash jr and sr after the Davis Cup 1986

The winning Davis Cup team 1986. From left: Mark Kratzmann, Neale Fraser, John Fitzgerald, Pat Cash, Paul McNamee, Peter McNamara, Wally Masur.

The celebration after the 1986 Davis Cup – Pat receives a spray from the captain

battle. 'I had prepared myself for the crowd, I knew exactly what was happening and it was exciting. No matter how much the Swedish people were screaming or the Australians, it wasn't going to put me off. I was prepared for it.'

Those privileged to witness the duel never will forget Cash's gems to secure the critical service break early in the fifth set . . . a running forehand down the line into the corner and a lunging stop-volley to a viciously

The Davis Cup dinner. In the foreground are Davis Cup stalwarts Larry Madison, Lyn Nichols and Stan Nichols.

topspun crosscourt forehand. In a comeback, unparalleled in Australia's distinguished Davis Cup history, Cash eventually overran Pernfors 2-6, 4-6, 6-3, 6-4, 6-3. The comeback was historic in the true sense, the first time an Australian had recovered from a two-set deficit to win the clinching match of a Davis Cup final. The importance of the historic fightback was starkly underlined when Edberg beat the still shell-shocked McNamee 10-8, 6-4 in the last match to reduce Australia's winning margin to 3-2.

At the Davis Cup dinner that night, Fraser, a captain not prone to individualise, looked back over a lifetime involvement in the international teams competition and declared: 'I don't think the Cup has been won in greater circumstances than those in which Pat won today'. Then he handed the microphone to Cash for a response to Prime Minister Bob Hawke's toast to the team. As if to emphasise the team theme again, Cash, with no prior warning to collect his thoughts, delivered a witty and emotional tribute to each of his Australian colleagues.

'People say I won the Davis Cup which is not true at all. When you looked back on that year it was very much an overall team effort. Macca [McNamee] played in every match, Peter Mac [McNamara] set up the win in New Zealand playing the best I've ever seen him. And Fitzy and I teamed in every doubles. It was very much a team effort and I was able to look good to finish it off. Sergio Tacchini bought out a T-shirt which said Pat Cash Twice Davis Cup winner. It said Pat Cash, Davis Cup, Australia. The Australia was small and it was obviously designed to be recognised as me being a twice Davis Cup winner. I never wore that T-shirt, I gave all mine away. I didn't like it at all. I thought it was in bad taste and I told them that too.' Team man right to the end. Yet, despite the emphasis on overall contribution, the 1986 final will always be remembered as Cash's Cup.

4 Problems

Panic crept up on Pat Cash as he eased from the hospital bed. His legs would not listen to his brain. Forget a tennis return, I'm a cripple who can't even negotiate a dozen steps, Cash thought, as he fought to overcome the simple first obstacle to his comeback . . . ten feet of floor space from bed to bathroom. 'Just one foot in front of the other, an inch at a time was the only way I could get there. It took me five minutes to make it to the toilet. That was the scariest moment I had the whole time of the back trouble, these bad thoughts came through my head.'

What Cash had endured was the excruciating agony of an injection under local anaesthetic to dissolve the bubble of a protruding disc in the lower back, a debilitating ailment which threatened his career in 1985. It was a year of turmoil and torment when Cash's world ranking crashed from a lofty seventh to virtual oblivion in the 400s. Back to junior days when a player is required to battle through two qualifying rounds in a day against the tour 'hackers'. Coach Ian Barclay is convinced that Cash matured during those long, lonely and uncertain months away from the international circuit. Cash's fate took him down several roads – and to a few dead-ends – from the moment he lost in the 1985 Wimbledon singles second round until his re-emergence in the first round of qualifying at Fort Myers, Florida eight months later.

Only the medical experts know how precariously Cash's entire sporting life teetered on the edge after a CAT scan at Melbourne's Epworth Hospital finally ended the months of frustrating uncertainty and confirmed fears of a herniated disc L4 and L5 in the lower back. Rather than have surgery, as some specialists advised, he opted for radical treatment: a single injection

Top: John McEnroe and Pat Cash, Wimbledon 1984.
Below: US Open 1984

with chymopapain, a drug which contains extract from the paw paw fruit. Such a procedure can be risky and has variable results. Had the injection treatment, completed while Cash was still conscious, failed, major surgery was the only alternative to enable him to engage in normal physical activities, let alone play professional tennis again.

Rather than become confused with complex medical jargon, permit Cash to describe the back injury in layman's language. 'It's called disc protrusion or herniated disc. The disc is round like a coin and pressure from the vertebrae bones comes down to squeeze the discs. In my case pressure forced it to bubble out the side, hit a nerve and made my back go into muscle spasms. Some people have it very bad with sciatic nerve pain down their legs too. Mine was at the worst stage but the legs were never affected.'

Cash first noticed trouble with his back at the end of 1984, a year when he burst to international prominence as a semi-finalist at Wimbledon and the US Open. Following the heady days of the 1983 Davis Cup triumph Cash was under enormous pressure to push on to recreate the glory of Australia's illustrious tennis past. Anyone who has played on the pro circuit will testify to a tough grind where absolutely nothing is taken for granted, least of all a tennis heritage, and only the present really matters. The teenager struggled early in 1984 with first-round losses on the clay of Rome and Paris. But he blossomed in June once he felt the familiar grass under his tennis shoes in England. Cash bullocked past Robert Seguso, Mats Wilander, Cassio Motta, Kevin Curren and Andres Gomez to the Wimbledon semi-finals before John McEnroe, the eventual champion, halted the march 6-3, 7-6, 6-4. Cash again kept his best for the big occasion at the US Open by defeating Ilie Nastase, Brad Gilbert, Todd Nelson, Greg Holmes and again Wilander en route to the semi-finals. He held a match point in the fifth set against Ivan Lendl before falling 3-6, 6-3, 6-4, 6-7, 7-6. At the conclusion of the titanic struggle, Cash threw his racquet into the crowd, claiming a spectator several rows back had called for it as a souvenir. Officials sympathised with the disappointed Australian – and hit him with the maximum fine.

The subsequent ranking hoist for the year from 38 to 8 again prompted misinformed expectations that he merely had to turn up to Kooyong in late November to collect his national singles crown. Unhappy with his court movement at the Australian Open after losing to Johan Kriek in the quarters, Cash decided to stay at home and join the Hawthorn footballers for their summer pre-season preparations. It was February, one of Melbourne's hottest months, and he supplemented practice with Ian Barclay and Mark Hartnett by joining the footballers in road work.

'I didn't know any of the players that well then, but they accepted me.

Training with Leigh Matthews at Hawthorn *

Not being a good long-distance runner, I was last almost every time and it wasn't until I had been doing it for about three weeks that I started to get really fit. They used to do a lot of hill work and I remember there was one steep climb on a hole at the Wattle Valley golf club. It goes almost straight up and they used to sprint up there, jog back down and sprint up again. I can do it now, but then I could manage only about four in a row before I nearly died. Four players would go at ten second intervals. I started about the middle group and ended near the end. I got slower and slower, I was dropping further and further back. I couldn't believe how hard they worked and I got really fit that way. I hadn't done anything apart from the on-court work, I hadn't done any really quick stuff ever.'

At least the intensive football training in the heat improved Cash's cardiovascular fitness for a first round tie in the 1985 Davis Cup against Yugoslavia in Split, the resort city on the Adriatic Sea. It was to prove no holiday as he lost to Slobodan Zivojinovic in four sets over three hours 45 minutes, played a five-sets doubles match the next day and then beat Marko Ostoja in the reverse singles. His body was screaming for rest by the time he had played successive tournaments in Europe immediately following the Davis Cup commitments – beaten by Mats Wilander in the semis at Brussels and by Joakim Nystrom in the quarters at Rotterdam.

'I went from a bouncy clay court to low-bouncing Supreme surfaces indoors and my legs were sore even though I was playing well. My back was getting sore after I lost to Wilander. That was understandable and wasn't really worrying me. After all, I had played so much tennis over three weeks following a two-month break. My back was stiff, but my legs were giving me the most trouble. Knowing more about the body now I realise that as soon as your legs get sore you start compensating, moving differently and put strain on your back.'

It was during practice at Harry Hopman's camp in Florida the following week that Cash's back flashed the warning signs. He felt sharp pain while doing a routine stretching exercise on the floor at Paul McNamee's apartment in Tampa, near Hopman's headquarters. 'I was lying on my back, pulling my knees up to my chest which is as simple an exercise as you can get. Then all of a sudden, bang, and I thought "what the hell is this". One side of my back went into spasms. I had a few days off and went to Houston to play a WCT event. I got to the quarter-finals at Atlanta the following week although I couldn't move. My back was stiff and I couldn't serve properly. That's when I knew there was something really wrong with my back, something I had to get fixed. The tennis trainer said it was just a muscle spasm. But the one I did at Macca's place was high up my back on one side and that disappeared. Then the lower back went into spasms.'

After resting for a week, Cash headed for a rich tournament in Las Vegas where he was one of the top seeds. The dice didn't exactly roll his way in casino city: a bad back complicated by an even worse draw, with hungry American Jimmy Arias first round. Arias won 1-6, 6-3, 7-6 in a battle of the

Caesar's Palace gamblers – Cash hoping his back would hold up and Arias clawing out of a career slump. 'I wasn't moving very well and I remember going back for a smash in the third set tiebreaker. I landed awkwardly and I really felt my back, it really hurt me. To that stage there hadn't been a lot of pain, more the discomfort of a tight back. At the time it didn't seem to be any worse until the next morning when it was stiff and sore. Sometimes you get stiff if you play a long match and I thought it was caused by my first match on hard court for a while. I had a day off before playing doubles with Fitzy [John Fitzgerald] and found I couldn't even walk comfortably. I found it uncomfortable to sit in a chair, tough to get my legs moving when I stood up and I couldn't straighten properly. When I played with Fitzy, all of a sudden I couldn't serve at all. I couldn't bend, anything lower than my waist was a gimme point.'

Despite the restrictions Cash refused to let down his Davis Cup teammate, particularly in such a rich doubles event carrying big money and computer points. So weak was Cash's serve that he always had the wind behind his crippled back to put maximum power into what normally was a major weapon. Against the odds, the Aussies reached the final to face American Paul Annacone and South African Christo Van Rensburg. 'I wanted to do well, we were a good team and I didn't want to default on Fitzy. My back was getting stiffer and stiffer because there is no chance to rest it when you're winning. Basically I had been hitting the ball better than in '84 and that was keeping me going. My footwork was bad because I couldn't move. But I was hanging in there and playing good doubles. Fitzy and I got to the final and I managed to get a guy to loosen up the back a bit with some massage cream. When I got out of bed on the morning of the final, I couldn't walk. We ended up winning 7-6, 6-7, 7-6 and there were only two service breaks in the match. Fitzy played a great game, he covered most of the court and I put in a few good returns. I was serving half pace but getting some decent volleys away. I was just sticking my arm down and hoping I would get the ball back. I couldn't move, bend down and get in the right position.'

X-rays in Houston showed no sign of bone damage, only a slight curvature in the spine, a result of the spasms pulling the muscles to one side of the body. At least the enforced break allowed him to pursue the long, leggy Norwegian model named Anne-Britt he had met at a party a few weeks earlier. The heart strings were in working order even if the back muscles moaned at every movement. Cash bypassed the Italian Open, choosing rather to test his back representing Australia in the World Team Cup at Düsseldorf. This time the confidence as well as the aching back took a hammering when he lost to West German Hans Schwaier in straight sets. He

Ian Barclay and Pat Cash 1986

Pat is congratulated by team-mates after defeating Brad Gilbert of the US in the 1986 Davis Cup semi-final

Renee, Patrick and Daniel
1978*

Pat with nephew, Lee Barnett*

Wimbledon action. Left: 1987
Above: 1983

admitted feeling hopeless. While he could get traction to push off on hard court or indoor surfaces in the US, now he was like a newborn giraffe which had wandered on to an ice-skating rink. So uncoordinated was Cash on the European clay that West German Claudia Kohde-Kilsch even believed she could beat him after watching the match on television.

'On clay I was just sliding with no control over my back and legs. It didn't feel as if my legs were part of me. I couldn't move at all and I was about as slow as a tennis player could get. When I tried to change direction I would just keep sliding and then it would take me ten minutes to get back. Claudia Kohde-Kilsch apparently saw me on television and said how she could beat me on clay. She was quoted as saying she could beat anybody outside the top ten and especially Pat Cash on clay, or something like that. She saw that I couldn't hit the ball over. I was trying to slide and almost clean missing, like a beginner. I wouldn't have been surprised if she could have beaten me. But I still didn't like the comment too much.'

Few tennis people other than fellow Australian players knew the mental and physical torment endured by Cash. So crisply was he striking the ball that it prompted him to press on, despite the restricted court movement. And when he couldn't perform up to self-expectations, he vented his frustrations on racquet, ball and the occasional linesperson, as the code of conduct violations piled up in the opening months of the 1985 tournament calendar. Like most of the controversy in his life, there was a reason if not justification for the seemingly irrational ravings which attracted the fines. The injury problems hadn't even surfaced in Australia although he could sense the media believed that the creditable Grand Slam performances of the previous year were merely an emotional highpoint of a young man destined to be retarded throughout his career by a suspect temperament.

The vindictive tongues wagged more eagerly when he pulled out of the French Open. Rumours abounded that Cash was scared of clay as he headed for the green grass of England and comforting, understanding Anne-Britt who was back home for a break from modelling in the US. To forget the injury woes, the pair flew to Paris as guests of film maker Michel Mattei who was making a movie of the Australian's life. 'He had organised a party for my 20th birthday with all his French mates. He did it all so well and had gone to so much trouble to organise a special party with tennis players and ex-champions. They like me in France and I felt a real rat because I had pulled out of their tournament. He had organised all this for me and I had to pull out of their event.'

Still hampered by back pain and stiffness, Cash also withdrew from the grass court tournament at Beckenham in Surrey and chose to stay in London to prepare for the traditional Wimbledon lead-up at Queen's Club in fashionable West Kensington. Back in England he had made a couple of visits to Terry Moule, an osteopath whom Paul McNamee even brought to Australia one summer to treat his back. Moule lived about 70 kilometres from London, a minor inconvenience for the desperate Cash who would gladly have travelled to the end of the earth for a cure . . . or even a diagnosis.

'Grass was my best chance and I was practising the day before Queens when I hit a serve. All of a sudden my back just went crack and everything tightened. I thought, "I've done it now". I could barely walk and couldn't bend to one side. I had been to see Terry a couple of times and I didn't have anybody to turn to. So Barkers called up Terry and we drove to see him. I was lying in the back seat with my legs up. It was so bad I couldn't sit up in the car. It was probably the worst thing to do because all the driving made my back worse. He gave me some treatment, cracked it a bit and gave it a rub. What was most frustrating was not knowing the source of the problem. They can't really tell about a disc by feeling your back. No body could tell me exactly what it was. There were all sorts of suggestions, everything from a spasm to curving in the spine and even one leg shorter than the other.'

Somehow Cash was still a viable foe as he beat Peter Doohan, Vijay Amritraj and Mark Edmondson, all fine grasscourt exponents, for a quarter-final against a young German kid named Boris Becker. 'My serve was about the only thing operating as I couldn't bend backwards because that was all stomach muscles. Most of the Aussies were aware of the back problem but they didn't realise how serious it was. I didn't really know who Becker was and I was hopeless. He beat me 4 and 4 which really didn't look too bad considering how I was feeling. Of course then it was a big upset because I had got to the semi-finals the previous year. It was when everyone started to ask "who's this Becker kid?" I was really the one who started it all off for him.'

Restricted by the back pain, Cash virtually had no practice before he faced big-serving American, Todd Nelson, in the opening round at Wimbledon. He struggled through the five-sets match so constantly interrupted by rain it was spread over three days. Qualifier Ricardo Acuna of Chile didn't let him escape in the next round after the dogged Australian had levelled the match from a two-sets deficit. Acuna won in five sets on Court Two, an enclosure which had earned a reputation as the graveyard of champions. Fitzgerald and the restricted Cash, who was still returning well, salvaged something from the doubles as they beat John McEnroe and Peter Fleming before eventually falling to Heinz Gunthardt and Balazs Taroczy in the final. 'I was seeing the ball well but I just couldn't move. I couldn't cross properly and couldn't intercept any of their volleys. Any bad returns and

Fitzy had to do a lot of the work and you just can't afford to team like that against top players. Looking back we did a fantastic job getting as far as we did.'

Cash remained perplexed by the back ailment as he headed home for a Davis Cup quarter-final against Paraguay in Sydney. He was examined in Melbourne by physiotherapist David Zuker and an orthopaedic surgeon. For a week Cash rested the back, lying at home for most of the day and moving only to visit Zuker for treatment. Despite stretching, traction and electronic stimulation through the muscles, the back failed to respond and the concerned medicos arranged for more thorough tests.

'I thought good, I'm getting everything checked. The treatment had relaxed me a bit and I was able to hit the ball okay, even though I still wasn't moving properly. So I packed all my bags for the trip to Sydney and drove to Epworth Hospital for the scan. I had to wait for the results and take them to Zukes. It was after-hours when I got there and walked upstairs. The surgeon and Zukes were sitting there and I thought it was a bit of a coincidence. Then Zukes said "sit down, you won't be going anywhere for a while". He told me I had a disc protrusion and would have to take a break. No running, nothing. The surgeon said it could take three weeks or three months. They told me to go to Sydney and watch the Davis Cup, give the boys support and take it easy. In a way it was like getting to the semi-final of Wimbledon. Not so much the happiness of '84 but a relief to get people off my back. I knew there was something wrong and everybody was giving me a bad time. I knew it wasn't my tennis and I was kind of happy in a way. It was the relief of knowing for the first time exactly what was wrong.'

The subsequent announcement that Cash was out of the Davis Cup team was the first inkling something serious was amiss with the nation's top tennis player. Speculation about his future flew as thick and fast as the yellow balls on the Sydney grass courts when Cash pulled on headphones, instead of the customary headband, as a television commentator for the Australia-Paraguay tie at White City. During that Sydney visit, Cash found the man – or, more correctly, the man found him – to start the long recovery. Sports fitness specialist Nigel Websdale, whose methods were as successful as they were unorthodox, basically wanted Cash to place emphasis on strengthening the lower back and stomach muscles to relieve pressure on the spine.

'He called me up on the phone and said he could fix my back. I said, yeah, yeah, and thought he was another guy looking for publicity and he talked me into having a meeting with him. I expected a physio, maybe in a tie. This guy walked in wearing a tracksuit, he had a front tooth missing and looked like a surfer. And he was. We went for a drive to a Sydney beach while he told me his life story. He was a muscular little guy, maybe 38 who looked 28. He had a set of exercises that he swore by and he gave me enough confidence to try his methods. Nobody had told me how to fix my back.'

Websdale convinced Cash that he had to strengthen the stomach muscles to support the back and introduced him to health foods; a diet that would let the natural process heal the body. It was a long term approach which required Cash to spend many hours in the gymnasium. Cash started the stretching work during a holiday with Anne-Britt at Port Douglas, north of Cairns on the north Queensland coast, before returning to Melbourne for another back scan to check if there was improvement in the disc. One of Australia's top neuro-surgeons confirmed that treatment was required to correct the problem. After consultation it was decided to attempt to rectify the ailment through the chymopapain injection, a solution which dehydrates the fluid in the sac bulging from the disc in the spine.

'The last thing I wanted was an operation, so they suggested the injection. I remember they drugged me up, wheeled me down and got me into position for the X-ray. Basically what happened was the guy gave me the injection and could see the needle going into the disc. Then they would release the stuff and check it on the X-ray. When they put the needle into my disc I thought I was going to die. I was moaning and I could feel my back go into spasms straight away. I was almost asleep and it was just like a nightmare. Then I thought "thank God it's finished" and they said, "right, now we're going to put the stuff in". I was in so much pain I almost passed out. The next morning I stayed in bed and eventually I was in hospital five days. I had been a bit sick and they were giving me all these injections which I thought were pretty good because they eased the pain.

'The first day I got up to go to the toilet. I was sitting on the edge of the bed and I put my feet on the floor and eased my way up. I was standing and I thought "right, I've made it". But my legs just wouldn't move, I couldn't walk. That's when I panicked. "They've done something wrong, I'll never be able to walk, I'm a cripple". But the guys came in and said they were going to treat it like major surgery, as if the disc had actually been removed.'

To speed the recovery Cash altered his diet to one similar to that of a body builder, with a high protein intake to promote muscle growth. He temporarily moved to Sydney to work out with Websdale and a chance meeting at the same clinic hammered home the realisation that patience really was a virtue under the circumstances. The example of Australian Test fast bowler Michael Whitney made it easier to accept. Whitney told Cash he needed three operations on his knee because he kept trying to come back too early.

'He [Websdale] was a great believer in hot baths and keeping the back warm. I thought I was a fish after a while. I was having three baths a day, doing everything he said. It was tough and I still didn't know whether to believe him. My dad didn't really believe him. He has the results but they won't believe it and I can understand why. It's real guru stuff. We worked to change my diet and I learned a lot about my body. At that stage Anne-Britt was pregnant and I was keeping that quiet, so it was a really weird period. I could see myself getting stronger but I didn't know if I could come back. At that stage, after a few months, it was getting to the anxious period. The Australian summer was coming up and I had to miss the Australian Open. It was a tough time for me, but then I gradually got stronger and stronger.'

To this day Cash has preserved the secret of Websdale's special exercises. 'I don't tell anyone what they are. I don't do them very much any more unless I have a lot of time. They put a lot of stress on your arms and your back, your whole body basically. It's a toning sort of thing. There was a lot of the stuff he was throwing at me that I couldn't handle. But I did whatever he wanted because I knew I had to get back.'

Cash moved the comeback headquarters to his London flat in January 1986, and found a small gym around the corner in Chelsea to continue the daily routine. He went there six days a week for three weeks and started off riding an exercise bike. The bike was on the lowest pressure yet his legs were so weak after an inactive five months he couldn't pedal for even ten minutes. For the three weeks in January his monotonous daily routine was to take a morning bath, go to the gym about midday, stretch for an hour, workout, then stretch for another hour and finish with a hot bath. He took another bath at the flat before falling into bed, limp and exhausted.

By the end of January Cash was raring to go again and he met Barclay at Hopman's camp in the US for three weeks intensive training. So keen was Cash to resume matches that he rang captain Neale Fraser to make himself available for the first-round tie in New Zealand. He arrived in Auckland with three weeks practice and an eight-month lay-off as his credentials for selection. 'I was so keen to be with the boys again that I got off the plane and went out next day to practise for four hours. After that I was so stuffed I couldn't get out of bed for two days. I was absolutely exhaused, as sick as a dog. I do that all the time, come out and go flat out, go too hard straight away. My work, my tennis, my gym work, whatever. Everybody keeps telling me to do it slower. Okay, I do it slowly for two days and then I'm like a bull at a gate again.'

Cash was so ill after the initial Davis Cup practice session that he had to be coaxed into playing the doubles rubber with Fitzgerald. Two days before the match Cash told Fraser and his teammates that he still felt bad. Buoyed by the team's confidence in him, Cash worked strongly over the next 48 hours and, with the reliable Fitzgerald by his side, the pair defeated Kelly Evernden and Russell Simpson 6-2, 6-3, 6-3 to give Australia a 2-1 lead in the tie. It was his first important match since he and Fitzgerald had lost the 1985 Wimbledon doubles final.

With his confidence partially restored and no sign of back pain, Cash headed to the US to start rebuilding a ranking which had plummeted to a lowly 413th, necessitating three qualifying-round wins merely to make the main singles draw of a major tournament. In search of a fitness adviser, he called up his old friend Ann Quinn, who had used Pat as a subject for physical tests when she was a student in human movement in Melbourne. Cash found her at the University of Illinois completing a master's degree which specialised in tennis fitness. Strangely, Quinn's thesis was based on the importance of abdominal muscles and the lower back in selected tennis strokes. The pair could only bemoan the fact that they were not working together before he was injured. Immediately she began to map out a fitness course to bring Cash back to an acceptable condition.

On his own admission, Cash bluffed through the first qualifying match at Fort Myers in Florida against American Dan Cassidy who had won the Victorian Open in the Australian's home town that summer. His form gradually improved as he beat Christo Van Rensburg of South Africa and Canadian Martin Wostenholme to reach the main draw. He knew he was on track despite losing to Aaron Krickstein 5-7, 7-5, 6-4 after squandering break points in two games to take control in the third set.

Equally ominous were the obstacles looming on that long road back to world status. He hit such a trough the following week in chilly Chicago, quitting a first-round qualifying match against Texan David Dowlen with the contest deadlocked at one set each. Cash explained the walk-off as the mixed emotions of one struggling to come to grips with the stark reality that a return to best form was months rather than days away. 'I wasn't too sure about my back. Even though it was indoors the weather was freezing. The other reason was I was playing so bloody badly. I didn't really want to go on anyway. I was in a filthy mood, frustrated and really mad at myself. I thought things were going well and all of a sudden they didn't seem so rosy. I took four days off and started practising for Atlanta where I had a wild card straight into the draw. I played Tim Mayotte first up and got beaten 4 and 3. It was a tough draw but that was my first real match.'

Deep down Cash knew he was back. The pain that winners experience in defeat bit into the gut rather than the spine. And he knew he could work off the leg stiffness with the daily running and stretching routine controlled by Quinn. Barclay was constantly on the practice court as Cash tried to quench the insatiable thirst for matches. The lower back agony was becoming just a painful memory.

5 The Cash Clan

When the international circuit swings Down Under for the Australian summer, Cash heads straight for the family home in North Ringwood, about 30 kilometres east of Melbourne's city centre. The house has a lived-in warmth to complement the views of the rolling tree-lined hills out the back, a swimming pool below and the tennis court a further level down. Cash's bedroom remains virtually untouched with an oversized ANZ Bank cheque pinned to a wall. The $15,000 first prize was the booty from his first Grand Prix singles crown in January, 1983. After winning that title he deposited the real cheque at the local Ringwood Branch the next day and went off to treat himself to a new set of headphones.

At 22, Cash is the eldest of Pat and Dorothy's three children with sister Renee two years younger and brother Daniel another year behind. All have been touched by tennis. Dorothy plays midweek competition, Renee was a member of Victoria's Wilson Cup squad and Daniel now gives coaching lessons on the family court. Dorothy had three children by an earlier marriage in the US and all have families of their own. Craig lives in Brisbane, Laura at Bacchus Marsh, a town west of Melbourne, and Ralph's wife and child are in New South Wales.

Despite the ten-year gap and the geographic spread, the Cash family remains a tight-knit unit. They were drawn even closer together when Ralph died tragically in August 1983 on the eve of Pat's departure to the US and, understandably, he wanted to stay at home to be with the family in their grief. His father and mother pleaded with him not to sacrifice plans to play the US Open and had to almost drag him to Tullamarine Airport to board the trans-Pacific flight. 'He died two days before I left to go to the States. I didn't even have a chance to go to the funeral. It was such a shock and it hit

Above: Pat and Dorothy with Daniel, Renee and young Pat *
Below: Craig, Ralph, Laura, Pat and Dorothy with Renee *

Daniel, Pat and Renee *

Prep. grade at Our Lady of Good Counsel. Pat is on the far left.*

us all around pretty badly. I had to go away and it didn't make it any easier at that stage, particularly when the pressure was on to do well.'

Imagine an 18-year-old alone in New York trying to lock his mind on to tennis, knowing the torment being endured back home. Not unexpectedly, Cash ran into trouble with officialdom, fined $1750 for twice throwing his racquet and abusing an umpire during a second round match against Glen Michibata of Canada. Inevitably, he lost third round to American Bill

Scanlon amid an outcry over un-Australian behaviour. Amid the torrent of criticism, even from his own countrymen, Cash decided to ride out the storm. He preferred to keep his suffering within, although he took the extraordinary step of apologising for his actions when he came home for a Davis Cup semi-final against France early in October. 'I was a bit tight at the time,' was Cash's guarded explanation of a stressful month. 'I've spoken to my family about it and that's it.' No doubt the family concern was a contributing factor to his fiery attitude at tournaments prior to and following the US Open. He was ignominiously dismissed from a special event at Port Chester, New York, following three code of conduct violations a week before the US Open, and then incurred a further fine during a tempestuous week in Brisbane before eventually beating Paul McNamee in the final to win the GWA Classic.

Although mellowing with age and often bitter experience, Cash will always retain an egalitarian sense of justice which lies behind most things he does. People who don't do the right thing by him cop it. If James Dean were to be reincarnated as a tennis player in the 80s, he would surely return as Cash. It all fits; the anger, the glamor, the sex-symbol, the feeling of being misunderstood. Cash admits to a stubborn Irish temper – the unbending independence from his mother's Chicago background and the rage which was transported with ancestor Martin to the colonies from Country Wexford.

Cash regaled a fascinated press contingent on a dull day at Queen's Club in London this year with a reason why he might have been labelled the Wild Colonial Boy of tennis. 'It's because,' he told them, 'I have a convict ancestor.' Cash's great-great-grandfather and Martin Cash, later to become a legendary Tasmanian bushranger, arrived in Australia at the same time from the town of Inniscorthy in Wexford, Ireland. There's no documented evidence that any Cash in Australia is a direct descendant of Martin, although it's possible the families are related. Martin Cash was, indeed, famous for more then merely robbing coaches. As his young namesake described it to the English tennis media, Martin was sent to Tasmania's infamous Port Arthur convict settlement for shooting his girlfriend's lover. He was the only prisoner ever to escape from the forbidding place, Cash said proudly, and he would have been hanged except that the governor's wife, Lady Franklin, led a petition for his pardon. 'He was really popular with women, you see, a real superstud,' he said. Cash pondered that for a moment, then decided to elaborate. 'I don't mean,' he hurriedly explained, 'that he was a stud in that he produced a lot of children, I mean . . .' To which a grinning Pom suggested: ' . . . that he put it about a bit?' 'Exactly,' beamed the boy from Ringwood.

Above: Pat senior with a very junior Pat*
Below: Pat helps with the dishes*

Anne-Britt, Pat and Daniel *

Such light-hearted banter was another example of the thaw in the previously icy relationship of player and press. There was a time when Cash would er and um his way through monosyllabic press conferences, distrustful of presenting his true personality. He is still unforgiving of those he considered have 'burned' him, although generally far more expansive with answers, perhaps mellowed by a beautiful girlfriend and an energetic son who help sweep away any on-court worries.

Norwegian model Anne-Britt Kristiansen walked into Cash's life at a low point of the Australian's tennis career when he sought treatment for his ailing back from a doctor in Houston, Texas, in 1985. According to Cash, party hosts Vitas Gerulaitis and a friend seemed to have mustered all the good-looking girls in town and the venue was wall-to-wall with glamorous models.

'I hung around with the tennis players and didn't know all that many people there. I was talking to a couple of Aussie guys when I was introduced to Anne-Britt. She was the most stunning girl in the place. She was talking to all the Swedish guys and said later that it was the first time she had spoken her language for about a year since she got to the States. Anyway, I thought she was well taken so I didn't bother about going and trying to chat her up or anything.'

When the back pain continued after a tournament in Las Vegas, Cash returned to the friend in Houston for treatment. To cheer him up the man-about-town medico took him to a nightclub where he spotted Anne-Britt with Gerulaitis' friend who had thrown the party. Cash was too shy to make an approach, so the young doctor boldly decided to test the water for him. 'So he just went up to her and said that a Mr Cash would like to speak to her. I didn't have an idea he was doing this and was just talking to someone else. She had wondered who this Mr Cash was. He must be a Texas oil millionaire, a big fat guy with a beer gut. The doctor tapped me on the shoulder, I turned around and there she was. We started talking and I wasn't going to let her go the whole night. So we made a date for the next night and it just went on from there.'

Anne-Britt's modelling career was progressing in the US as her new admirer kept in touch from Europe. She was infatuated herself and admitted that her interest in the catwalk and cameras waned when the Australian left for London. Cash telephoned and asked her to come to England as his guest with the stipulation that she would have to go home or stay with a friend once the championship business began. 'So she came over and ended up staying the whole of Wimbledon, five weeks instead of two. We fell in love before I went back home and found out that I had to rest my back and take a holiday. When they gave me the bad news she was the first person I thought of, but she was just at the beginning of the summer clothes season and had a lot of jobs organised. She didn't want to come over at first but I talked her into it.'

Anne-Britt arrived in Australia the day after the Davis Cup quarter-final

Young Pat, the night before he left for his first overseas tour in 1979 *

against Paraguay in Sydney at which Cash worked as a television commentator. After meeting the rest of the Cash clan, the happy pair headed for the beaches of north Queensland to soak up the sun . . . and to become better acquainted. 'That's when she became pregnant with Daniel. It was a total accident. Originally I just freaked out because that was the last thing I wanted. Everything was up in the air. I didn't know what was going on with my back, my ranking was going down the tube and I really wanted to get back and start doing a lot of work. Now I had a pregnant girlfriend who I had only been going out with for about four months.'

Back in Melbourne the young couple decided against consulting the family doctor who was the father of his mate Mark Hartnett. Instead they sought out another nearby medical practitioner and Cash waited in the car while Anne-Britt went for the examination. 'She went in there by herself and I waited outside thinking, "I don't really want this. I'm only 20, I don't really want to have a baby". Obviously, she didn't either, what with a career and trying to work. It just wasn't the right time at all. Then I saw her walk out and say goodbye to the doctor. She came towards me and I asked. She nodded her head, yes, and I thought "oh hell". Then she burst into tears. For a week she was downstairs in her room crying. She was away in Australia and couldn't talk with her Mum or Dad about it. She didn't know what she was going to do. The folks didn't know until I told Dad. I thought he would have a heart attack, but he was very cool under the circumstances. He was really excited, over the moon that he was to become a grandfather. Actually I was talking to Dad when Mum came in the study. She said "Oh, sorry, I didn't realise" and Dad told her to stay. He announced that Anne-Britt was pregnant, Patrick and Anne-Britt are going to have a baby. She said "That's nice, are you going to get married?" and I said no. She asked why not and I said because I don't want to and she said okay and walked straight out of the room. My brother and sister were excited and we had made up our minds to have the child. It wasn't as if I couldn't take care of him and didn't have the money.'

For five months the pair kept the family secret as he worked in London and Melbourne to overcome the back injury. Eventually Cash realised the game was up when a noticeably expectant Anne-Britt appeared in a bikini poolside at Palm Springs in California where he went to test his back by playing doubles with American left-hander Tim Wilkison. The reporters' questions were diverted from the back ailment and first round defeat to baby speculation. Coach Ian Barclay and Cash fended the queries until he telephoned his father in Melbourne and it was decided to announce the joyous news. Cash sought out freelancer Richard Evans, an Englishman who he trusted to put the story into the right perspective. Soon the news of Dan-

Pat, Dorothy and Pat sr *

iel's development was zinging through the world's communication wires. Still, it was greeted with scepticism when Cash reached Auckland for the Davis Cup first round tie.

'The boys all stopped practising and we were having a chat. Then Macca (Paul McNamee) said "gee, Cashy, you've had a rough time, just got over your back and now they are putting in the papers that Anne-Britt is pregnant". When I told him it was true, his jaw nearly hit the ground. Nobody could believe it, they didn't know what to say. My immediate thought was that, like you see in the soap operas, people might believe she had tricked me into it. Being close to Macca, I told him the whole situation. It's hard to describe, it was one of the worse times of my life trying to get my ranking back and yet also one of the best. I was really over the moon and excited about it.'

As the predicted date of arrival edged closer, Cash found himself wrestling with a tough decision. He beat Tomas Smid and Jakob Hlasek, two fine clay court players, in the World Team Cup in Düsseldorf before losing in three sets to Joakim Nystrom. He resisted the temptation to accept a wild card into the French Open and every day booked a flight to Oslo under a different name. Teammates McNamee, Peter McNamara and John

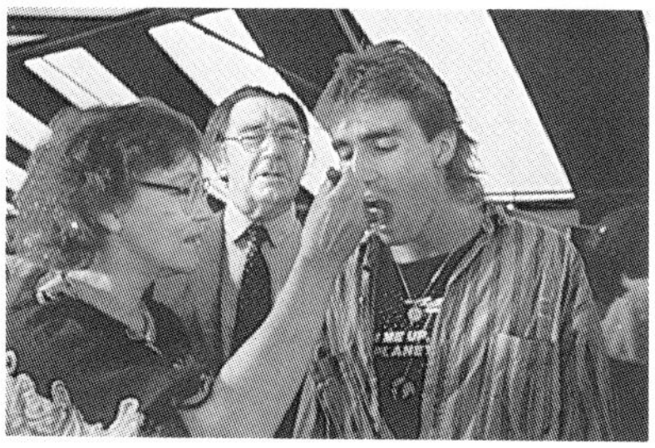

Top, bottom and opposite page: Pat's 20th birthday party at the French Open 1985.

Fitzgerald realised that Cash would be on his way to Norway at the first signs of labour. He fulfilled a promise to be there for the birth.

'There was a lot of excitement at 10.30 at night when she started to get contractions. Daniel was born at 2.03 the next morning which was my 21st birthday. I was in the room with Anne-Britt and she was only in actual labor for about 15 minutes. Bang, he just came straight out, didn't want to hang around. It was the greatest shock of my life, I actually jumped backwards. It was both scary and fantastic and I wouldn't have missed it for anything. My 21st birthday was the longest day I have ever spent. I stayed there for a couple of hours and then went back to the Kristiansen's place at about four o'clock and collapsed into bed for four hours sleep. When I came back from a visit to hospital, they had a birthday cake ready for me. I drank about a bottle of Bailey's to celebrate.

'For a while I was just like a kid with a new toy. To me he was the most beautiful thing I had ever seen. He didn't become really interesting until three or four months when he started grabbing things, smiling all the time. That's when my life started changing. I thought this is the real stuff. Obviously it's a lot different at home, it's a lot more fun than just sitting around. But it has also created problems because it's not easy travelling with a baby. At one stage he was six months old and I hadn't seen him for half his lifetime because I was travelling. I couldn't believe the change and I felt really bad. It was tough to look after a little baby. I was training harder than ever at that stage and Anne-Britt was going crazy. We realised it was very hard to travel with a baby all the time but we are learning from experience. We've had our ups and downs, it hasn't been easy, but I think we are learning. It costs a lot of money but I wanted them to be with me. They are my family now.'

Fortunately, while Anne-Britt was still in the Oslo hospital for post-natal care, Cash lay in a similar London medical centre convinced he was dying. Five days after the birth of his son, he doubled over at home with appendicitis. Melbourne friend Rocky Loccisano, a pennant player trying his luck on the satellite circuits, was staying with Cash at the Chelsea flat and drove him to nearby St Stephen's Hospital. After tests for a swollen oesophagus, gall stones and an ulcer, the appendix was finally pinpointed as the culprit. With Wimbledon only a month away, the doctors told Cash he could delay the operation and get through the championships on medication. But they warned his training would inevitably suffer. 'I told them I couldn't play like that. I called up my Dad and he said "I think you should have the operation, it's bad luck but let's get it over and done with".'

It became a delicate operation to avoid damaging abdominal muscles as much as possible. 'Normally they put it right down in the groin area, just cut

the muscle and pull it straight out. The surgeon made it a bit higher. There are three sets of muscles that go across the area in the stomach and he went through a little hole in the muscles and pulled the appendix through, like a keyhole operation. The muscles gradually came back together and were as strong as ever after a couple of weeks. I had been doing strengthening exercises for my back and had super strong stomach muscles. I was on the exercise bike at the hospital within a day and doing gentle sit-ups.'

Australian tennis mate and practice partner Charlie Fancutt eventually convinced Cash that he had nothing to lose by accepting a wild card invitation to Wimbledon's main draw. Before the appendix attack, Cash snr had requested a wild card which was certain to be granted considering his son's fine record at Wimbledon. Now Pat had to convince tournament referee Alan Mills that he was fit to play by providing daily reports on practice progress. Only two weeks following the operation, Cash played Mats Wilander in a charity match in Dublin. Mills was satisified. On a severely limited preparation, Cash beat Guillermo Vilas, Russell Simpson, Jay Lapidus and No. 2 seed Mats Wilander to reach the quarter-finals. Eventually the lack of fitness caught up with him against flashy Frenchman Henri Leconte in four tight sets. His leap from a gruesome 413th to 102nd was the greatest single tournament advance in the history of computer rankings. Equally important was the reassurance for corporate backers. 'It had been more than a year since I had more or less won a match and the companies were asking "what the hell is going on". Some were basically ready to dump me. They are in the business of selling racquets and clothes and if I'm not on court advertising them, why should they pay me. I don't blame them at all. Those championships saved more than my ranking.'

To Cash it became blatantly obvious he required specialist training and Ann Quinn agreed to assist the recovery. He understood that the operation had caused him to run out of steam at Wimbledon and didn't want it to happen again. Quinn had cancelled her trip to London following the appendicitis attack and their serious training began when the tournament circuit swung to the US. She drove Cash hard, at times to the point of exhaustion. Often he trained for more than three hours before a match in a bid to become the fittest player on the circuit. Despite indifferent form in the US, he made the semis of the Australian Indoor in Sydney, beat John McEnroe first round at Wembley and was a semi-finalist at Hong Kong to boost his ranking back into the 20s. Following Cash's brilliant form in the Davis Cup final at Kooyong, most expected he would carry it through the 1987 Australian Open a couple of weeks later. Other more experienced tennis observers like Neale Fraser knew he would be struggling to rise again only two weeks after such emotionally-draining Davis Cup commitments.

Unbeknown to all except those closest to Team Cash, the intensive work backfired within reach of his own national singles crown. He felt pain in the right shoulder after mis-hitting a couple of shots in the quarter-final against Yannick Noah. 'I had done a lot of work on my serve and my shoulder just fell off. My shoulder was killing me and I served only three quarter pace in the semi against Lendl. It was just overuse and there was nothing that would fix it except rest. I won that match somehow, just because I volleyed so well. It was a dry court and the ball bounced high so I was just rolling my arm. I got a lot of stick off the serve, it came off the court quickly. The next day before the final I couldn't practice at all. I saw Zukes and he loosened it up. Strangely, the shoulder felt great for the first two sets and Stefan [Edberg] just wiped me off the court. Then it got sore as I got back into the match. Near the end of the fourth set I was up two breaks and served three doubles in a row. My shoulder was so weak I was serving like a girl. I was trying to get a bit of extra power and I lost my rhythm altogether. I wanted to hold that serve and try to break early in the fifth. By blowing that, it probably cost me the match.' Cash fell just one set short of the perfect Australian summer as Edberg wriggled out of trouble and instead helped himself to the early service break in the deciding set to win his second Australian singles crown 6-3, 6-4, 3-6, 5-7, 6-3 in three hours 40 minutes.

By that stage Cash had begun work with sports psychologist Jeff Bond. While Quinn, who also works with other clients such as Olympic skiers, is on a retainer and is now more available to travel the tennis circuit, Bond flies in for only the major events such as Davis Cup, Australian Open and Wimbledon. As with his coach Barclay, Cash has unquestioning faith in his advisers.

Quinn carefully maps out his day: when he eats, exercises, practices, plays and winds down. She monitors everything he consumes in the low fat diet of vegetables, fruit, grilled meat and fish and a minimum of dairy products. Rarely do they train at a tournament site, preferring to find a deserted court to undertake the strange but specific routines such as dashing to corners to collect the strategically placed yellow tennis balls. Cash and Quinn grin when they watch other players attempt to copy the routine because it's so precise that it requires the correct drop of the knee at the right time. So secretly do they guard the work that Cash often varies the workout if they suspect someone is spying.

Cash's verve for super fitness has encouraged others to follow the lead and, for instance, Davis Cup teammates John Fitzgerald and Wally Masur now travel with an adviser, Sydney fitness expert Steve Johnson. Fitzgerald asked Cash a question about his off-court routine during the Davis Cup quarter-final in Brisbane in July this year. The reply was courteous and

SERGIO TACCHINI

curt, not surprising when you consider the teammates could become foes again the next week in a tournament. Such is the individualistic nature of the sport that every player closely protects training routines. When Cash ran alone some mornings on a track beside the Brisbane river, he carried in one palm a written set of instructions to remind him of specific tests. And the quest for ultimate fitness was emphasised, following each of his singles victories over the Mexicans. Cash ran the three kilometres back to the team hotel after beating Leonardo Lavalle. And, with nine aces and 60.5 percent of first serves finding their mark in ten untouched service games against Jorge Lozano, the Australian went straight to the practice court for 45 minutes – to work on his service rhythm.

Bond's value is more intangible: a calmer Cash who now can handle the disappointments and distractions of a match situation. He said the secret was to find happiness in your game, to go out there and feel happy when you are playing. I realised that the umpires make mistakes just like I do. I'm a fiery person and if I yell at them, they get their backs up. We made up our minds that when they make a bad call, talk to them instead of yelling at them. It's very hard for me to do in a big situation. You try and stay calm and not get hacked off at a bad line call. As it turned out at Wimbledon,

there was hardly a bad line call in the whole tournament for me.'

More and more, Cash will rely on his entourage as a shield from the press and public who, naturally, want to pry into the inner thoughts of a Wimbledon champion. He has watched how time and again a seemingly insignificant comment from John McEnroe or Boris Becker has been twisted to suit a newspaper headline. 'It's disappointing because I like to have a chat and a joke. But it's no joke when I get misinterpreted as at Wimbledon. I said that when I'm 34 I want to be down at the beach drinking beers with a mate. Very tongue in cheek stuff and I find it was in the sports section in New York the day after that I like going down to the pub with my yobbo mates. The Aussie guys at the press conference knew I was joking and put it in the right perspective that I do like to have a drink with my mates and a good time at the appropriate time. Instead the others had me an alcoholic. I have to be guarded and I'm going to have to think twice otherwise it will be in a headline.

Whether it's interpreted as naivety or honesty, Cash has always attempted to treat people equally, irrespective of their stature in tennis. A story retold by *Tennis Australia* editor Alan Trengove at the 1984 US Open illustrated Cash's distaste of pomposity. It involved two interviewers eager to learn more about the Australian who had beaten Mats Wilander to reach the semi-finals. As Trengove retold the story: 'Almost simultaneously, Chris Martin, a young London radio reporter, and a slick CBS television type buttonholed Cash on his way back to the dressing room. Martin is a battler, a freelance who works almost around the clock trying to eke a living from the sport. One of his customers is an Australian radio station. Though he had interviewed Cash before, Martin hardly knew him. The CBS man, however, had behind him the power and influence of a vast network which pays millions of dollars for the TV rights to the Open. When CBS want anything at the Open – an interview, a certain centre court schedule or a courtside mike to pick up the players' arguments – they get their way. The CBS man imposed himself on Cash, insisted he went to the CBS studio immediately for an interview that would be seen by millions. Martin trailed behind. Then, at the studio, Martin asked if he could come inside to hear what was said. The CBS man brushed him off. Cash was already inside the studio. Suddenly he'd had enough of the American bluster. "I'm going to talk to the other bloke first," he announced to the CBS people, leaving them looking startled as he joined an equally startled Chris Martin outside the studio.'

It tells much about Cash. He is tough-minded although not unbending. I recall a similar situation during his advance on the 1987 Wimbledon crown. London-based Australian radio journalist Mark Fogarty sought Cash for a short interview immediately following the main press conference at which

Pat has been playing the guitar for quite a long time *

the Australian had explained the quarter-final victory, coincidentally, over Wilander. My request to eavesdrop in the stuffy, small radio room was granted. A weary but relaxed Cash, clad in baggy shorts and T-shirt, even agreed to introduce his own interview with a snappy wake-up call to be sent down the line for a Melbourne breakfast show. And with darkness descending outside, he sat back for another 20 minutes to discuss the theory of his psychology work with Bond, the new member of the team. Given the time and treated with respect and dignity, Cash is a willing and forthright interviewee. Unfortunately, such informative chats will become more infrequent as the clambouring attention which, sadly, accompanies the spoils of Wimbledon triumph, forces a retreat behind locked doors.

Imprisoned in hotel rooms and relying on room service, Cash finds solace in his music. Where possible an electric guitar is packed away in the luggage with an expensive headphones-amplifier system. The small box allows feedback of his own strumming which is super-imposed over the sounds of a cassette through either the headphones or mini speakers. Theoretically, he can practise the guitar while baby Daniel sleeps undisturbed in the next room.

'I have this friend Mick Cocks who started me off with the guitar. He used to play in Rose Tattoo a long time ago and there's another guy Mark Evans who used to be in AC/DC for a long time. They have had several bands together and now have one playing in the pubs in Sydney. I'm good mates with them and they teach me a couple of songs every time I get up there. They are in a band called the Rolling Clones, they do the Rolling Stones covers and they are great. They're really good musicians and I admire them. I really love guitar music and one of my biggest ambitions is to play like these guys. I really want to play properly. I want to play it just for the sake of being able to play well and to enjoy it. The biggest thrill I've ever had, apart from tennis and Daniel, was to get up on stage and play with my mates in Sydney one night. The most I've played before would be about 200 people. It's a different sort of thrill to tennis.'

6 Wimbledon

For a moment the rock-steady concentration waivered as Pat Cash turned and nodded for the boy to release the two yellow tennis balls. The overflowing Wimbledon centre stadium crowd and millions of television viewers held their collective breath. Slowly Cash raised his steely grey eyes to target the world's No. 1 player Ivan Lendl, who stood in a menacing crouch at the other end of the court. Already Cash had watched the second seed survive four consecutive critical points to stay alive in the opening set tiebreak and now he stood at 6-5 with a last chance to consolidate a vital lead. For the first time in the entire 13 days of the championships, Cash was consumed by self-doubt. 'Negative thoughts came into my head as I heard the umpire say 6-5 and the crowd's oohs and aahs. As I collected the ball to serve, I thought of losing the set and quickly told myself "No way. Right, here we go, first serve a big serve right in the corner". I pictured myself hitting a great serve right in the corner and did exactly that.' Cash's unplayable bomb exploded on Lendl's backhand, the ball crazily ricocheted off his opponent's racquet frame to seal the opening set of the 1987 Wimbledon men's singles final after a gripping 73 minutes.

'The serve was perfect, the greatest relief of all time because I knew I had to get that first set. I thought I would win if I got the first set. If I hadn't then it would have been a real struggle.' Armed with a brutal serve, Cash blasted the dispirited Lendl 7-6, 6-2, 7-5 in two hours 45 minutes of sustained power to claim his first Grand Slam singles title. It was a spectacular way to end Australia's 16-year drought on the world's most famous tennis stage and become the first Australian to win the men's singles crown since John Newcombe in 1971.

What most impressed tennis watchers throughout the championships was Cash's control – not merely of his game and his opponents but his mind. He was calm in press conferences, declining any brash predictions, content to take one match at a time. By deciding not to play doubles he was able to be away from the claustrophobic confines of the jammed All England Club walkways, away to practise with coach Ian Barclay, run with fitness adviser Ann Quinn, take a walk in the park with Anne-Britt and Daniel or to revise the mental homework with sports psychologist Jeff Bond.

Bond taught Cash mental exercises to prepare for a big match; to go to bed at night and imagine situations that may disrupt his rhythm, such as a bad line call or a stalling opponent. The theory, according to Cash, was that he had then already decided the best way to handle that obstacle if or when it did loom in his path to glory. The Australian Institute of Sport psychologist occupied an upstairs bedroom at Cash's new home to be right on hand to conduct the counselling sessions.

'Usually Jeff and I would have a chat the night before. If I was nervous then I would chat to him before a match. Each night we had something to work on and think over. One of the main things was to pull my concentration back when I was losing it. We would do a quick relaxation thing, just to get me loose. Deep breathing, lying down on the couch or bed so I could think clearly without worrying about what I was going to eat the next morning. Then we would go through aspects of a coming match. I would think about them before going to bed so they were in the mind, in the subconscious.'

To remain fresh during Wimbledon, Cash went against the wishes of Barclay in deciding to bypass the doubles. It was tentatively arranged for him to team with big Yugoslav Slobodan Zivojinovic until the Australian insisted on a single-minded approach. 'It can be too heavy a workload for one day; a five set singles and then you have to come out an-hour-and-a-half later and play a best-of-five doubles. You could possibly play ten sets in a day and have to come up fresh the next. It's impossible, even if you are not that physically sore or tired. Mentally you are a bit slower. I knew this time it was much more important to be fresh.'

Frankly, his build-up to the championships had not been idyllic. A back scare, and the persistent rain, cast a damp pall over what was to be a fine-tuning week. Cash became concerned when he felt twinges of back pain during a practice session at Queen's Club and his father Pat senior left nothing to chance after receiving the troubled telephone call in Melbourne. He immediately contacted physiotherapist David Zuker who had supervised the recovery following Cash's spinal disc problem two years earlier. Zuker was on the first available flight for the 24-hour trip to London and a surprised Cash awoke one morning to find his friend anxious to start prodding and

Sergio Tacchini
Sergio Ta

poking the suspect lower back region. To everyone's relief, Zuker found nothing more than the expected stiffness.

England's soggy summer start wasn't so easily overcome. Cash and Barclay kept the kilometres ticking over on a loaned car, as they scoured the countryside in search of a playable grass court. Several times they made the journey to Surbiton, south-west of London, where Cash is a member, only to find the courts too treacherous for play. Absolutely no consolation was the fact that every other Wimbledon contender in the British Isles was, to use a term befitting the conditions, in the same boat.

'The weather was a worry as it had rained every one of the 20-odd days we had been in England trying to prepare for Wimbledon. I was hitting the ball well at Queen's and I just needed to tone up on a few things – returns and passing shots mainly. When you don't hit a lot on grass, you don't get the timing and and just end up pushing the ball around, not hitting through it confidently. It was just a week for fine-tuning and I still didn't know how I was going to play. It depends a lot on the draw. You might play someone whose style you don't like. I knew if I played well I had a chance. As it turned out, I played better than I thought I would.'

Four days before the start of the championships, Cash gave the first clear pointer that 1987 just might be his year. In the mad scramble for practice courts, Cash and tall American Tim Mayotte were pencilled in for one hour on Court 15 as the overcast skies hovered ominously. Watched by a handful of curious onlookers from the Debentures Lounge window overlooking the outside enclosure, Cash shaded the 10th seeded Mayotte in a spirited serve-

volley duel before setting off for a gallop through the nearby Wimbledon common with Quinn. 'Don't work him too hard,' ordered Cash senior, perhaps sensing that his boy was ready.

'I had practised with Tim and a few other players indoors, but it was the first time since Queen's that I had played someone of that calibre on grass. I specifically tried to get big-servers to get my eye in on the returns, because I needed work on that facet of my game. The way I played against Mayotte gave me a lift. Going into that practice I wasn't sure of my form. You have an idea of the serve and volley, but the returning game is just as important on grass.' To hold control over such an accomplished grass court exponent as Mayotte became a ray of sunshine, otherwise absent in the damp atmosphere.

Few others believed Cash could win. The bookies shops were offering 16 to 1 before his first round match against little American Marcel Freeman. 'Freeman was tailor-made really because he wasn't a big-server and I could get my eye in on the returns. He hit the ball hard and was basically a solid all-round player, but nothing spectacular. But everyone is a danger player who can give trouble if they get a run on. I was pretty nervous going into that first round. In fact I was anxious for the first three matches as I didn't have much idea how I was hitting the ball, I couldn't gauge myself.'
Cash defeated Freeman 6-0, 6-3, 6-2.

Of more concern was a second round confrontation with his good pal and Davis Cup teammate Paul McNamee. The effusive Australian, with his deft change of direction, pace and lightning reflexes at the net, can totally dictate the game if allowed to play in his frenetic fashion. And the match was on the No. 2 "show" court which, for reasons best known to its victims, had become the graveyard of many aspiring as well as established champions over the years. McNamee, 10 years the senior, worried his protege in an opening set which contained five service breaks. Once past that test, Cash utilised his power to blast aside the gallant McNamee. When Cash reached into his kitbag to engage in the now familiar dispensing of headbands, cheeky McNamee decided he wasn't going to be upstaged this time. As Cash tossed headbands into the stand, McNamee drew a roar of approval when he dug out a grubby sweatband and flung it into the crowd.

'I was anxious playing Macca because he knew my game so well. He is not a straight-forward player, you have to watch out for different shots. He is a player who can be great if he gets on a roll. I was nervous about that because I tried to get on top of him straight away and couldn't. We hadn't seen much of each other the week prior to the tournament and we were having a chat about the football results back home before we went out to play. I know I wouldn't have been too friendly if he had beaten me, but I think he believed deep down that I would beat him and what he wanted was to have a good shot at it. I don't think he was disappointed because it was a tough match.'

Cash defeated McNamee 7-5, 6-4, 6-2.

Dutchman Michiel Schapers was the foe in the third round. Cash remembered how Schapers ousted Boris Becker in the second round of the 1985 Australian Open on the same court surface. No repeat this time as the Australian overcame the heat, a code of conduct warning and a mid-match hiccup for a place in the last 16. Cash copped the code of conduct warning – his sole indiscretion of the championships – for an audible obscenity during the sixth game of the third set which had got away from him. After committing two errors, he turned away towards the baseline fence, raised an arm to mop the brow and shouted his frustration. The armpit wasn't offended but a baseline judge took him to task and reported the words to the centre chair umpire. Cash didn't allow the incident to snap his concentration, seizing an early service break in the fourth set and clung to it doggedly.

'After three weeks of miserable weather all of a sudden this one day was just unbelievably hot and humid. I was dying on the court after half-an-hour of practice. My shirt was soaking before we had finished the hit-up prior to the match. It just drained me so quickly that after the first set I was really struggling to get power in my shots. I lost concentration through exhaustion in the third set and got mad with myself. I fired up in the fourth set although I was still struggling to find my form. That type of match can really knock you into form, a tough three or four set match. It's the best tonic you can have when you are out of form . . . so long as you get through it, of course.'

Cash defeated Schapers 7-6, 6-2, 2-6, 6-4.

Like a portent of doom for allcomers, Cash sounded the warning siren from faraway Court 13 in the fourth round. He was simply untouchable in blowing away French left-hander Guy Forget. Those who ventured to the 'show' court tucked away in the corner of the All England Club grounds nearest Church road, witnessed a transformation in the young man who had struggled and occasionally stumbled through the soggy opening week. Gone was the lethargy and uncertainty. Cash's absolute authority so unnerved Forget that he threw in four double faults in the fourth game. Like colleague Henri Leconte, Forget was armed with heavy artillery but had the same propensity to shoot himself in the foot.

The Australian's dominance was aided by an outrageous winner in the eighth game of the third set. Trailing 3-4, Cash raced back in to retrieve a perfectly placed Forget lob and only had time to make an underarm flick at the ball. The Frenchman, poised at the net for the kill, watched in dismay as the Cash miss-hit ballooned over his head and landed on the baseline.

'I had returned well in the first three matches but couldn't find consistency on the serve and volley. That's what I concentrated on this time and it worked out well. I had cramped after Schapers match and, knowing I had to come up again the next day, I was watching the telly hoping Forget would have a long doubles match. I knew I had to improve on that day's performance against Schapers to beat him because, obviously, the further you go, the tougher the opponent. Forget has got an unbelievably fast serve, one of the fastest I have seen, so I wasn't that super confident of beating him. I was just hoping that he would serve a few faults and I would get on top of it. That is exactly what happened.'

Cash defeated Forget 6-2, 6-3, 6-4.

So awesome was the Cash control against Swedish ace Mats Wilander in the quarter-final that it prompted a prophetic appraisal from a man with an intimate knowledge of what was required to win Wimbledon. When the Australian swept through the opening set, Gunther Bosch, the coach who steered Boris Becker to glory on the same centre court the previous two years, turned to a commentator and remarked: 'There is your new Wimbledon champion'. Blunt testament to Cash's dominance was that he dropped a mere 19 points in 16 service games. Four were conceded in the second game of the third set to lose serve for the only time in the 130-minutes centre court romp. No panic when trailing 0-2. Cash summoned the inner calm to re-generate the concentration and lost only one point in the next four service games. 'There was nothing more I could do,' the despondent Wilander said. 'He returned my serve so well too, all I could have done to improve was hit aces.'

'From the Schapers match to the Forget match I think I improved about 75 percent', said Cash. 'If I had to gauge it, I would say I was 85 percent against Forget and probably 99 percent against Wilander. I knew I had to serve well against Mats because he was a bit sick of the game when I played him at Wimbledon the previous year and it wasn't a good guide. This was a big match, I served harder and more aces against Mats than against Forget because I knew I had to. Against Wilander I was moving so well, covering the court so he couldn't get the ball past me. I knew if I could beat Mats I had a great chance.'

Cash defeated Wilander 6-3, 7-5, 6-4.

Finally Cash had earned a break after three consecutive match days and he immediately called up compatriot Brad Drewett to help prepare for the semi-final against Jimmy Connors. He had a minor scare during a 90 minutes workout when he strained a muscle at the top of his right buttock. But a massage, an ice-pack and electronic stimulation of the muscle by a trainer in the locker room alleviated the problem. Certainly, there wasn't a chink in the mental steel which had blocked out every possible distraction throughout the championships.

That armory came under intense fire late in the second set of his clash with Connors. As the supercool Cash served to wrap up a two sets lead, Jimbo finally latched onto a couple of deliveries to awaken the centre court crowd. When the veteran Connors ripped a forehand return down the line to break serve for the first time, the stadium echoed to a deafening roar. Memories of Connors' comeback from near death against Swede Mikael Pernfors on the same court two days before prompted hope of another great escape. But the young man from Melbourne required only a couple of minutes to lull the crowd back to polite applause. In one of the finest pieces of turnabout tennis, lost to most amid the seemingly effortless scoreline, Cash faced the danger and beat it to a pulp. Imagine the feeling of a packed house willing an opponent to overrun you. What no report can vividly capture was the sheer bravado of Cash as the pumped-up Connors served to square the set at 5-5. In the shock and disappointment of not serving out the set, it would have been understandable for the Australian to run and hide. Instead he rocked Connors right back on his heels by attacking his serve, storming the net behind a sliced backhand or viciously topspun forehand.

It was the dual Wimbledon champ who eventually cracked with a double-fault before Cash again rushed the net behind a second serve to punch away a crosscourt forehand volley. Watching the second set snatched away again squeezed the last ounce of resistance from the defiant Connors as twice more he surrendered serve. A rare standing ovation from the Royal Box, led by Prince and Princess Michael of Kent, was as much in admiration of Cash's mastery as bidding Connors farewell. Cash senior wasn't surprised. He ventured to the locker room prior to the match to find Pat feeding his son. 'Daniel was on his knee with pasta and sauce everywhere. He was very relaxed,' reported the contended Grandad.

'I was pretty annoyed to let Jimmy off the hook in that second set. If he had got that he might have powered through. But I knew I had him if I got it; he couldn't come back again. What was so good about the whole of Wimbledon was that I bounced back quickly every time I was broken. That's what Jeff [Bond] and I worked on . . . as soon as you lose concentration, tell yourself to wake up, let's go. Some players lose concentration for an entire set whereas ideally you should pick it up within

one point. I was happy to get the Connors match over as he was playing better at the end. He started clowning around with the crowd and made it very tough to serve the match out. The umpire seemed to have less control and I felt like having a word with somebody about it. That's what the 15 second rule is all about, to be fair to both players, and the umpire let it go altogether. Also the crowd was right behind him hoping for another comeback and it makes you a bit edgy.'
Cash defeated Connors 6-4, 6-4, 6-1.

Realisation that he was through to the Wimbledon final didn't prompt Cash to alter the meticulously planned tournament routine. A quick rubdown, the mandatory press conference and then 'just get the hell out of there'. Bond always had the car waiting and the plan was to get home, relax and slip back to normal family life. Right to the end Cash protected his privacy and sneaked out for a last practice workout with fellow Australian Darren Cahill at Surbiton on Saturday while most people at the club were inside watching the women's final on television. At the stroke of two o'clock, Cahill was ready to tone Cash for the last obstacle the next day.

On Sunday morning Cash awoke to a special pre-match breakfast of unrefined complex carbohydrates, cereals, fruit and grained bread. He even had a special formula drink beside his chair during the final – fluid that he had not become reliant upon but more as another psychological plus – to know that the energy boost was at hand if required. One hour before the final was time for a short warm-up with Cahill on Court Six: just to loosen up, get the blood circulating through the legs and release the butterfly colony which seemed to have nested in the stomach overnight.

'By the time I walked on court I felt good. They used to lock the players in a little room while everyone was sitting down but they didn't do it this time. We just stood in the corridor. He [Lendl] was in one corner, I was in the other and so I didn't really see him until we walked out. Everything seemed a bit more intense whereas there was a jolly atmosphere at the semi-finals. All of a sudden you realise "this is it". The day before they had organised which seat I would take beside the umpire's chair, all the towels I wanted were there, the ball boy took my bag out, everything was preplanned. I had been on centre court plenty of times but this had never happened before, so it was a little strange. It would have been better if everything was exactly the same, although it wasn't too bad. By the time I walked out on court I was feeling good.'

Apart from the traditional about-face and bow to the Royal Box on reaching the service line, Cash didn't take another backward step for the afternoon. He bombarded the tournament second seed with power-laden

serves, giving up only six points in six games before the inevitable tiebreaker. Again the sheer weight of the deliveries and blistering returns, particularly off the backhand, became the telling factor as he surged to 6-1 before Lendl rallied to 6-5. In the chilling silence Cash rocketed a first serve wide to Lendl's backhand to clinch the critical lead. Sniffing victory, he launched another blitz – parcelling up the second set without dropping a point on serve – and survived a slump in the third set. Lendl was poised to extend the match into a fourth set when he served at 5-3 before a double fault let it slip. The Australian gratefully accepted Lendl's fascination with serving to his lethal backhand and simply continued to drill winners past the increasingly frustrated Czech-born finalist. Cash fired volleys to his opponent's shoelaces, as if trying to rearrange his ankles, and broke serve again for a 6-5 lead. Powering through the 12th game, he clinched victory with a crosscourt forehand volley before triumphantly raising arms at the realisation of becoming the 11th Australian to win the Wimbledon mens's single crown.

'By the time I hit the first few balls in the warm-up I felt great. Lendl just looked more nervous after I started well. The first service game is critical to get you in the right frame of mind and I was seeing the ball well from the beginning. Normally it takes you a set to start getting your eye in. But I got straight into the groove and hit a few winners which rocked him a bit. I felt so comfortable on my serve and it was consistent. The court was so fast and I think he was a bit surprised how well I returned considering the surface. I didn't know until later that I hadn't dropped a point on serve in the second set.

'When he broke serve it really pissed me off that I didn't break straight back when I had 40-0. I had a bit of a downer for a couple of points, missing two volleys. The mind did wander because it was going a bit too easily at that stage. I was just trying to play a solid game instead of going for my shots. I got a little negative and just pushed the ball back hoping he would make a mistake. I realised straight after I lost serve what I had done wrong. I was willing him to make mistakes instead of forcing them and straight away I went on the attack again.

'After match point it was more like I couldn't release myself from concentrating. I felt happy instead of hysterical. I think I had done all my thinking, all my planning, all my dreaming the day before the match. When I had actually done it, it was like *deja vu*. It's really hard to explain, nobody can understand it. It just didn't feel like I had won the championship I had always wanted, that I had always dreamed about. Jeff said that was understandable because I was still concentrating on my performance.'

Cash defeated Lendl 7-6, 6-2, 7-5.

As the centre chair umpire dutifully observed Lendl's last rites and announced the score, Cash suddenly felt compelled to share the magical moment with The Clan. Defying 101 years of protocol, he vaulted the green courtside wall into the stand and, in a trek reminiscent of the last scene in *Crocodile Dundee*, clambered over the applauding spectators to reach his family and friends in the competitor's box about 10 metres above the centre court. He hugged and kissed his closest fans in an emotional outpour of jubilation. Staid old Wimbledon had never seen anything like it. Normally the players don't dare move from their courtside chairs until Their Royal Highnesses, the Duke and Duchess of Kent arrive to present the trophy. The crowd loved Cash's spontaneous sheepdog climb of victory celebration and the startled Wimbledon officials silently tolerated it . . . this time, anyway.

'It was just something I wanted to share with my family and a few people in particular. My father, Barkers, Anne-Britt and in a more professional way Jeff Bond, Anne Quinn and an English buddy of mine, Geoff Lamb. There was my stringer up there too, Derek May, who lives about 100 miles out towards Bristol. Every day he drove in, collected my racquets, took them home to string them and brought them back next morning. He ended up stringing about 14 racquets each day. If it was eight I would find four that were exactly right and the others would be too high or low in tension. It was his last Wimbledon after doing it for 20 years. He had strung all the champions' racquets, Laver, Newcombe and so on. But I was the first one for whom he had actually strung the racquets from the beginning, who went on to win the championship.'

In a moment of jubilation Melbourne barrister Brian Cash lifted the distinctive black and white checked headband from his nephew's forehead after that unconventional visit to the competitor's box. The evolution of this strange item of headgear provides a pointed insight to this remarkably determined Australian sportsman. The headband design signifies the chequered flag, the ultimate target for which he turned up the turbo in that sleek body for the two hours and 45 minutes required to complete the race of his tennis life.

Uncle Brian discreetly returned the pilfered headband at a party organised for a small group of family friends that night at Cash's home in London. No fancy five-star hotel reception room for this down-to-earth hero. He merely wanted somewhere to mentally unwind with his mates . . . in private. Cash's message to those invited was simply 'make yourself at home and grab a drink until I get back'. Resplendent in black dinner suit, the new Wimbledon champion took Anne-Britt, his family and friends to the plush Savoy hotel in The Strand for the traditional Wimbledon victory

Melbourne gives the Wimbledon hero a civic reception

dinner. The ample stocks of Foster's cans was dwindling when the champ finally returned to the sanctuary of his living room again at about 11.30 pm. Out of the stuffy but smart suit and into shorts and T-shirt, he began to ease down the adrenalin flow. Into the early hours of the morning, the casual Cash moved among the 30 guests including fellow Australian players Cahill, McNamee, Nicole Provis, Jenny Byrne and Davis Cup captain Neale Fraser. The gold replica of the All England Club's Challenge Cup, quaintly inscribed 'The single-handed championship of the world' stood virtually unnoticed and untouched on a book case.

'I wanted to enjoy myself without waking up with a headache. I wanted to have a chat with everyone but I didn't want popping champagne, screaming and yahooing around. I felt I had done the work. We would have a bit of fun. But it was nothing to go over the moon about. I felt pretty humble and wanted to keep my feet on the ground.'

The enormity of what had been achieved . . . and a minor disappointment to accompany it . . . struck Cash a week later when he returned to Wimbledon to finish filming a documentary on his life. Each champion's name is inscribed on an honour board on the wall to the right inside the members' entrance of the All England Club.

'It was the first thing I looked for when we went back to finish off the film. I walked straight in and it wasn't there. Each winner is in gold embossed writing and they hadn't had time to get it up. I really wanted to see my name up on that board. I think it might be there now. The next time I go back I'm going to check it out.'

The exultant Cash, Wimbledon 1987

The climb to The Clan

The Cup presentation by the Duke and Duchess of Kent

The homecoming,
Melbourne July 1987

7 Postscript

Four days rest and reunion with Anne-Britt and baby Daniel in Norway immediately following Cash's heady fortnight at the All England Club replenished the energy supplies. But nothing could prepare him for the added burden of having the tag as Wimbledon champ precede him to tournament sites, particularly as he embarked on a mission to lay to rest the theory that he couldn't play on hardcourt. 'I didn't feel the expectations to do well, I just felt the attitude was a little different from my opponents. It was either one way they had nothing to lose or usually the other way as soon as they did start losing, or if I got on top of them early, they kind of threw it in. A lot of them just went for their shots. I wasn't all that familiar with hard courts because I had missed tournaments early in the year through injuries and various things. I was a little bit lost with exactly how I wanted to play, so that put me in a bit of trouble at times.'

That devil-may-care attitude of opponents and recurrence of tendonitis in the right knee retarded Cash's hardcourt education in the US late in 1987. According to Cash, young Andre Agassi hit every line, to beat him 7-6, 7-6 at Stratton Mountain before Swede Peter Lundgren brought the doubters to full voice by downing the struggling Australian at the Canadian Open in Montreal and the US Open at Flushing Meadow. The knee soreness flared during intensive training in Montreal and eventually a cortizone injection helped relieve the pain. But he was ordered to rest for five days which interrupted preparations and practice for the US Open.

A ten-day holiday on a beach near Cairns in northern Australia failed to alleviate the knee soreness which flared again when he returned to Sydney to resume practice on grass for the Davis Cup semi-final against India. The tell-tale strip bandage beneath the knee cap went, if not unnoticed, at least not queried in a rain-interrupted build-up by the Australians to face Ramesh Krishnan and the veteran Vijay Amritraj. Even when both teams filed into the hotel function room for the official draw, no-one outside captain Neale Fraser and his team realised that Australia would go into the first day of the tie without the reigning grass court champion. Buoyed by Cash's absence the Indians seized both singles with Amritraj, part-time tennis player, part-time businessman and forever the diplomat, smiling and caressing his way to a critical four-sets win over Wally Masur. Australia never recovered as Cash re-emerged from his self-imposed sidelining to help pull back a point in the doubles rubber. But nothing could save the hosts on the final day as Krishnan won again to clinch an upset 3-2 win. No-one was more distressed than Cash, a man who places only his family before national tennis duties. He rested the suspect knee for the hardcourt grind ahead, genuinely believing that Masur and John Fitzgerald could hold off the Indians.

To the relief of the tournament promoter, Cash decided to play the Brisbane indoor championship as the top seed and, naturally, the main drawcard. The white strip of cloth not only constricted the knee but more importantly his renowned verve for attack. Doctors advised Cash that, although the knee may be painful, there was no immediate danger of further damage to the tendon. But it was a tenatative and unhappy Wimbledon champion who fell third round to local back-court specialist John Frawley. By the time Cash and Barclay reached Sydney the following week for the Australian indoor championships, the bandage and those negative thoughts were discarded. 'I thought what the hell. If I'm going to worry about my knee, I'm not going to be able to play very well anyway. So let's not worry about it at all and just go for it. If my leg falls off, well, it falls off. I went out and trained really hard. I tore around the court like normal and it didn't really hurt anymore. I felt much more confident in my moving once I had done a few really hard workouts with Ian. Then I really played well there.'

For the first time Cash began to chip away at the wall of doubt built on the broken pieces that lay scattered from past hardcourt failures such as the second round defeat to Agassi at Stratton Mountain, third round to Lundgren at Montreal and first round at the US Open, again to the Swede. On the pale blue Plexipave at Sydney's Entertainment Centre, Cash simply waited on the short ball before advancing to punch away those low volleys that are his trademark. He served notice of a resurgence by beating tough little Kiwi Kelly Evernden first round, no mean feat considering the New Zealander had won the lead-up event in Brisbane the previous week. After wreaking revenge on Frawley and disposing of tall American Scott Davis in

a straight sets quarter-final, he faced second seed Boris Becker in a superb struggle that extended into the early hours of Sunday, finals day. With top seed Ivan Lendl safely tucked away in his hotel bed, Cash finally subdued Becker 6-3, 2-6, 7-6 in a match of the highest quality and drama. So sore were Becker's legs the next day that he was thankful he didn't have to be the one to face the world's No. 1 in the final. A fresh Lendl never let the lethargic Cash into the match, claiming the crown 6-4, 6-2, 6-4.

'You can't play a three hours match, finish around midnight, get six hours sleep before coming up against the number one player in the world and expect to give him a run for his money. I don't know why they schedule the semi-finals like that. The winner of the second one is always disadvantaged. I didn't feel that bad in the final, just took a while to get going and by that stage it's too late. You can't afford to let anyone get going; certainly you can't give Lendl a head start. That was basically it, I gave him a head start and he just got his nose in front and never let me into it.'

Indoor tournaments in Brisbane and Sydney were the start of Cash's concerted effort to rid himself of those hardcourt woes. An exhibition series in New Zealand and a special event in Antwerp were designed to prepare him for major indoor tournaments in Paris and London that he believed would secure the seventh of the eight places in the Masters field. 'But in London I realised I was in trouble for the Masters. I beat (Jonas) Svensson first round, then (Andrei) Chesnokov and I was playing better and better. Then came that close match against Anders Jarryd when that shocking line call cost me more than just one match. Jarryd went on to reach the final against Lendl. I really felt that it could have been me there and that would have sealed a spot in the Masters. When I lost I realised the only way to make sure of getting in was to go down there.'

Call it naivety, stupidity, whatever, Cash genuinely believed the trip to Johannesburg would not detract from his aim to end another long Aussie drought at Madison Square Garden, just as he had done on Wimbledon's centre court last July. Not surprisingly, he was granted a wild card by tournament director Keith Brebner and was met at the airport by a representative of International Management Group. A local sponsor also assigned a couple of burly minders to stay close to the first Wimbledon singles champion to visit South Africa for several years. As controversy raged in the Australian media, Cash flew to Johannesburg to follow a long line of compatriots such as Rod Laver, Roy Emerson and John Newcombe who made the southern capital a regular tennis stopover. Amid the furore, rarely was there mention of seven other Australian players such as Mark Woodforde and Simon Youl who had arrived for the same South African championships.

Even Cash was not prepared for the backlash he endured simply by extending his 1987 tournament schedule to stopover in South Africa, a Men's Pro Council Superseries event, on the way to his US goal. By playing a sanctioned tournament on the men's calendar, Cash became the subject of newspaper editorials and even a mild rebuke from Australian Prime Minister, Mr Hawke, a great admirer of the Aussie fighting machine beneath that distinctive black and white headband. To put the matter into perspective, an Australian public opinion poll published at the time showed overwhelming support for Cash's right to play in the South African Open.

'Obviously we knew there might be something funny going on and so I put up a big defence to the media when I first went there. I didn't know what to expect. I only knew what I read in the papers, people being killed and riots. I probably expected riots down the street and people trying to burn down the tennis stadium. We had a house with a court where we could practice all the time so we didn't have to go to the stadium and be bothered by anybody. After the initial press reaction we had a ball. It was just an incredible buzz, everybody wanted to see me. It was like they had been desperately waiting for me to come down, as if I was the only person in the world that could actually play tennis. I made a lot of friends there. It was lovely weather and I didn't see riots in the street. The only thing I ever saw were the little black ball boys and girls dancing and singing around me and kissing me. All they wanted me to do was give them an autograph, give them my headbands. I gave out all the headbands and the kids were just going crazy. Nowhere else except at home do I get a reaction like that from the kids at a tennis tournament. They were so excited to see me and it just really blew me over. That's why we decided to do something for them, to bring a couple of kids out to Australia.'

It was announced to the crowd after Cash beat American Brad Gilbert 7-6, 4-6, 2-6, 6-0, 6-1 in the final that the Wimbledon champion had decided to sponsor two junior players – one black and one white – to be brought to Australia for coaching under Barclay. In a statement read out by the South African Tennis Association President, Cash made it clear that his offer was so that 'players of all races will be in the forefront of tennis in the country'. Gilbert was so moved by the gesture that he decided he would do the same in the US. Once more Cash was the subject of thunderous applause and a standing ovation. 'The interest in tennis there is incredible and it was just one small thing I wanted to do. I almost felt sorry for them because they had been starved of tennis. They've got some great tennis players. I would like to see what the reaction is towards the tennis now. I hope it has helped a lot of people to go out and play tennis, black kids, white kids, whatever.'

Should he become embroiled in a similar frenetic Masters race this year, would he make the South Africa stopover again? 'I just don't think I could. There's no reason why I shouldn't, it's an official tournament down there. Any tennis player in the world can go down there and a lot of them have. There's no reason why I shouldn't but I don't think I will. Most people were right behind me, understanding that it was part of my living, one of my goals in life to play in a Masters final. In a way it's like playing Wimbledon, if you get the chance to play you don't pass it up. That's what it was like for me to get into the Masters. Most people realised that but there's always others who want to make it something sinister and bring politics into it. By going to South Africa doesn't mean I'm for apartheid, in the same way as going to China doesn't make me a communist. I don't agree with apartheid. I've never been that sort of person. Anyone who knows me can tell you I've never been a racist. The protestors should be getting on the people who put on the tournament, the Men's Pro Council. They are the people to blame for tennis players going there, not us. It's a sanctioned tournament and when Gilbert decided to go, of course I'm going too. I'm not blowing all those months of work by staying away from a sanctioned event.'

Emotionally wearied by the anti-apartheid backlash and coming off his 10 weeks hardcourt crash course, Cash drew a tough group at the Masters, confronted by Stefan Edberg, Mats Wilander and Miloslav Mecir. He lost tight matches to the Swedes and beat Mecir in the last of the round robin series. Obviously one win wasn't sufficient to reach the semi-finals and, thankfully, he headed back to Oslo to rest with Anne-Britt and Daniel. 'It was another achievement in my career. To win Wimbledon, to be part of a winning Davis Cup team, to play Davis Cup for your country and to play the Masters are all in the same group of elite events. So it was very exciting to go there and to play a competition which was as red hot as you could possibly get. Straight after the Masters, Anne-Britt, Daniel and I went back to stay at Anne-Britt's flat in Oslo. I spent about 12 days there and it was fantastic. We were a real little family for the first time in our lives and I didn't want to leave. I could have stayed there all year but I knew I had to get back to Australia and, more than anything, get acclimatised. I was jogging in the snow in Oslo and then I had to adjust to the heat at home.'

Cash physically peaked for another tilt at that cherished national singles championship. Fitness adviser Ann Quinn drove him through the torturous series of tests again – and found him faster and stronger in all of them. So eager was the Melbourne boy that he finally broke the 10-metres standing sprint time, much to his delight. That had gnawed away at him for more than 12 months. The hardcourt at the Cash family home nestled in the foothills east of Melbourne was re-surfaced with the Rebound Ace synthetic rubber

to duplicate conditions confronting players for the first Australian championships at the recently-completed $70 million national tennis centre at Flinders Park, less than a kilometre from the city's business heart. Even on a sunny Christmas Day, Cash was belting balls on the court, adjusting to the Nassau ball that didn't please him and the medium-fast Rebound Ace that did. Peter McNamara, appointed coach for the national tennis centre, pushed Cash hard through match practice sets as the rest of the competitors scrambled for the 21 courts at Flinders Park. Significantly Mats Wilander was the only player invited to the Cash home to practice when spare court time was at a premium during the heavy match traffic in the first week of a Grand Slam championship.

Unbeknown to Cash, Tennis Australia President Brian Tobin, after consultation with State Government officials, had signed a six part agreement with the secretary of the Australian Anti-Apartheid Movement in a bid to minimise disruptions during the championships. Understandably, Tobin, an International Tennis Federation representative on the Men's International Professional Tennis Council, was attempting to safeguard as much as possible the opening day of the championships when the hometown Wimbledon champion would make his first appearance. When the Cash family learned of the agreement – which included permission to roll tennis balls on court so long as it didn't interrupt play – they believed that Australia's No. 1 player had been 'sold out' to the demonstrators to ensure a smooth opening to the centre.

Brandishing placards, the small pocket of chanting protestors were strategically placed behind the court in the sell-out 15,000 seats main stadium as Cash made his centre court debut to a collective roar that would have shaken the revolutionary retractable roof had it been closed. Drowning amid the waves of Cash adulation sweeping the stadium, the protestors breached the agreement guidelines by tossing about 20 large black rubber balls on to court during a change of ends in the first set of Cash's match against Thomas Muster of Austria. Perhaps the anti-apartheid enthusiasm was dampened by the hostile reaction from the tennis public, as the demonstrators didn't return for the rest of the tournament. To escape with a single disruption was more than officials could have hoped . . . but the Cash clan didn't share their elation. Pat Cash senior clashed angrily with Tobin in the president's office with Davis Cup captain Neale Fraser becoming enmeshed in the argument. And Cash was seething when he came off court from a match he regarded as genuinely fraught with danger given Muster's creditable ranking and hardcourt prowess.

'I knew that something was going to happen. People had made a bit of noise in Adelaide the week before during the Rio Challenge and they got booted out by the people who had paid $15 to come and see good tennis. The funny thing was that two days before Wally Masur and Mark Woodforde had played the South Australian Open final. Both had been to South Africa and no demonstrators turned up then. So far as I was concerned that summed it all up. I really don't know what went on during my first match of the Open and then after the match Dad told me what had happened with the agreement. I couldn't believe it. Brian Tobin is one of the guys who voted to put the tournament in South Africa and now he's making agreements that could disrupt my matches. To allow people to throw things on court is just heading towards terrorism in my opinion. It could have jeopardised my chances of doing well in the Australian Open. I thought why don't they go and stand outside Brian Tobin's house and protest. Henri Leconte was there and he didn't get a protest. So were all the other Australian players who went to South Africa. Anyway I decided I wasn't going to let it bother me, but afterwards when I thought about it I was pretty mad. Basically I felt I had made my stand in South Africa very clear with the offer to bring two juniors to Australia. It was a diplomatic and friendly way to get the point across. To go there, collect the points and money and come back and sign a document blasting the system wasn't my way of doing it. South Africans would have regarded it as hypocrisy and it would have made no impact.'

All the Clan clustered around young Pat in an operation which bore striking similarities to Wimbledon. As at the All England Club, Cash confined his appearances to playing matches, giving a press conference and getting out of the place. Sports psychologist Jeff Bond stayed at the family home, and even his London friend Geoff Lamb rejoined the entourage. They could be spotted sitting together during each match – the expressionless Barclay, Bond, Quinn and Lamb. A few seats away was Cash senior, with that familiar body twitch each time his son struck the ball, as if the twang of gut on cloth sent an electric current through the body. Without conceding a set Cash disposed of Muster, Carl Limberger, Paul McNamee in an emotional night match, Jonas Svensson and Michiel Schapers to reach top seed Ivan Lendl in a semi-final showdown. A roar of the magnitude generally reserved for the Melbourne Cricket Ground just across the railway tracks erupted at the packed tennis centre when the home favourite downed Lendl 6-4, 2-6, 6-2, 4-6, 6-2 in three hours and 56 minutes. Standing between Cash and that crown was cool Swede Mats Wilander, the only other player in the tournament who had practiced on the private court.

With his last ounce of strength, Cash fought to hold on to a dream. But the fairytale that was to have crowned Australia's Bicentennial opening of the new tennis centre ended in a 6-3, 6-7, 3-6, 6-1, 8-6 defeat as Wilander

claimed a third singles title. In a four hours and 28 minutes epic that was always going to be decided on a couple of critical points, the tennis gods decreed it would be Wilander. With the stadium lights ablaze and the crowd at fever pitch, Cash crept within two points of his goal when receiving serve at 5-4 and deuce in the fifth set. But Wilander held his nerve and serve to stay alive. Eventually the weary Cash dropped serve in the 13th game and the unshakeable Swede gratefully served out to love.

'I just lost my spark a little towards the end of the fifth set whereas against Lendl I was moving better and hitting the ball better in the fifth set than anytime in the match. Against Mats I was just a little slow on the volleys and he passed me a couple of times. I was disappointed to have lost, but I went out there and played pretty well and it was really an exciting day to play in front of that crowd, it was really good fun. I couldn't have tried any harder than I did.'

Only when Cash's challenge had ended did the protective Barclay tell him of the telephone threats leading to the final. Barclay's wife Jackie had taken one call at an Adelaide hotel during the six-man exhibition the week before the Australian championships. She was told that unless Cash signed within 24 hours an agreement that he wouldn't play in South Africa again, his career would be cut short. Barclay received another call at his Melbourne home in the first week of the tournament threatening his family. The silver-haired father of three decided to remain silent to keep the pressure off the star pupil and took the precaution of asking security guards to keep watch over them during each visit to the tennis centre. 'Barkers told me after the final. I couldn't believe it. That is the lowest form of life and very gutless.'

While the tennis watchers dissected the final the next day, Cash put up his bloodied and blistered feet in a South Melbourne recording studio and clamped on the headphones. With well-known Australian musician Mick Cocks, he put the finishing touches to a record. 'We finished all the vocals and my guitar. Mick is going to finish everything. I would love to do a video if I can find the time. It would mean coming back to Australia to do it with the band.' The A side of the single is a cover version of an old rock classic and the flip side is a song written by Cash and Cocks. Not surprisingly, it relates to everything in this remarkable young man's life, a motto he takes with him to toe the baseline on tennis courts around the world. The song is called 'Do It Right'.